A FEW WORDS IN THE MOTHER TONGUE
POEMS SELECTED AND NEW
(1971-1990)

A FEW WORDS IN THE MOTHER TONGUE

Poems Selected and New
(1971-1990)

IRENA KLEPFISZ

THE EIGHTH MOUNTAIN PRESS
PORTLAND · OREGON · 1990

Grateful acknowledgement is made to the editors and publishers of the following periodicals, in which the new poems in this collection were first published: *Ikon:* "Warsaw, 1983: *Umschlagplatz*," "East Jerusalem, 1987: *Bet Shalom*"; *Sinister Wisdom:* "I cannot swim"; *Moment:* "Fradel Schtok"; *The Women's Review of Books:* "*Etlekhe verter oyf mame-loshn*/A few words in the mother tongue"; *Bridges:* "Warsaw, 1983: *Umschlagplatz*," "*Der mames shabosim*/My Mother's Sabbath Days"; *Tikkun:* "'67 Remembered," "Fradel Schtok," "*Etlekhe verter oyf mame-loshn*/A few words in the mother tongue," and "*Di rayze aheym*/The journey home" appeared in *The Tribe of Dina: A Jewish Women's Anthology*, Kaye/Kantrowitz and Klepfisz, eds., Beacon Press (1989).

Grateful acknowledgement is made for permission to quote from:
"Claiming an Identity They Taught Me to Despise" by Michelle Cliff, copyright © 1980 by Michelle Cliff, from *The Land of Look Behind* by Michelle Cliff, reprinted by permission of the author and Firebrand Books.
"Notes of an Immigrant Daughter: Atlanta" by Melanie Kaye/Kantrowitz, copyright © 1982 by Melanie Kaye/Kantrowitz, from *Nice Jewish Girls: A Lesbian Anthology*, Evelyn Torton Beck, ed., reprinted by permission of the author and Beacon Press.

Publication of this volume is made possible in part by a grant from the Oregon Institute of Literary Arts. The author offers her thanks to the National Endowment for the Arts for a grant which supported the writing of some of these poems.

Library of Congress Cataloging-in-Publication Data
Klepfisz, Irena 1941 -
       A few words in the mother tongue: poems selected and new
    (1971-1990) / Irena Klepfisz ; introduction by Adrienne Rich. -- 1st ed.
          p.   cm.
       ISBN 0-933377-07-X (cloth) : $22.95. -- ISBN 0-933377-05-3 (paper) : $11.95
    PS3561.L388F4   1990
    811' .54--dc20   90-3682
                                                                        CIP

Book cover by Marcia Barrentine
Book design by Ruth Gundle
Manufactured in the United States
First Edition 1990   10 9 8 7 6 5 4 3 2 1

Published by The Eighth Mountain Press
624 Southeast Twenty-ninth Avenue
Portland, Oregon 97214

For Shoshana Różka Lodzia Mamma Lo — in short
far der mameshi
Rose Perczykow Klepfisz

A FEW WORDS IN THE MOTHER TONGUE
NEW POEMS (1983-1990)

ACKNOWLEDGEMENTS

IN 1982 IN THE "ACKNOWLEDGEMENTS" OF *KEEPER OF ACCOUNTS*, I WROTE: "...I want to remind myself and others of the circumstances that are most conducive to creative work. A block of uninterrupted time—unencumbered by a job or financial anxiety—is critical to every form of creativity and rarely available to those of us who are out of the mainstream. I feel particularly fortunate to have received it... and do not want it to be taken for granted."

Since the publication of that book, I have been again fortunate in having such blocks of time. These were in part created by writer-in-residence grants from the New York State Council for the Arts and a National Endowment Fellowship Grant in poetry. These periods were extended and, in a couple of instances, new ones created by individuals who have continued to believe in my writing. I am indebted to my mother Rose Perczykow Klepfisz and my friends Esther Hyneman, Melanie Kaye/Kantrowitz, and Linda Vance. For ongoing support and very valued friendships, I am indebted to Evi Beck, Rita Falbel, Gloria Anzaldúa, Marianna Kaufman, Clare Kinberg, Lee Knefelkamp, Myra Leysorek, Christian McEwen, Bernice Mennis, Jean Millar, Lil Moed, Lilian Mohin, Lucille Saner, Susan Sherman, Stan Silverstone, and Judy Waterman. Their support strengthened my confidence to continue experimenting, finding new directions for my poetry.

Preparing and finalizing this manuscript required time, energy, creativity, and patience. I am indebted to my publisher Ruth Gundle, to my mother, to Clare Kinberg and to Judy Waterman for extending themselves and being willing to reread material and give editorial comments, to do the mechanical work of proofreading and reconsidering ways of presenting these poems. They helped enormously when deadlines were pressing.

Writing these words in the spring of 1990 in New York City where 70,000 homeless remain uncared for, I am even more aware than I was in 1982 of our society's stubborn ability to throw away human life, human potential, human creativity, to suppress the best in us, the art in us. I am conscious that the opportunity to write poetry, to have my work valued and presented to the public is hardly encompassed by the word "fortunate" and that my experience is extra-ordinary.

Introduction

To inherit an uninterrupted and recognized culture is a privilege. at very least, it shows you what you have to struggle with, as person and as artist, like a strong parent who both teaches and browbeats, can be learned from, stormed away from, forgiven, but whose influence can never be denied. Like a family from which, even in separation, you bring away certain gestures, tones, ways of looking: something taken for granted, perhaps felt as constriction, nonetheless a source, a point of departure.

Until recently North American poetry has largely been written by people who have possessed—or assumed—that privilege. More and more, in the late twentieth century, it is being written by those who do not. This does not mean that such writers—men and women of color, gay and lesbian poets, poets born to a language other than English, poets writing in the upsurge of the women's poetry movement of the past twenty years—have started in cultural poverty, or that a privileged culture confers unlimited advantages. But the relationship to more than one culture, nonassimilating in spirit and therefore living amid contradictions, is a constant act of self-creation. The life of North American poetry at the end of the century can be seen as a pulsing, racing convergence of tributaries—regional, ethnic, racial, sexual—which, rising from lost or long-blocked springs, intersect and infuse each other while keeping the strengths of their origins. (A metaphor, perhaps, for a future society of which poetry, in its present underground and marginalized existence, is the precursor.) All this, as the official culture and institutions decline, sapped by extremes of profit, dishonesty, and fear.

Irena Klepfisz's work is an essential part of this poetry of cultural re-creation. It begins with a devastating exterior event, the destruction of European Jewry in the Nazi period through the technologically organized genocide known as the Holocaust, or, in Yiddish, *der khurbn*. (Klepfisz has written: "The Yiddish word was important, for, unlike the term Holocaust, it resonated with *yidishe geshikhte,* Jewish history, linking the events of World War II with *der ershter un tsveyter khurbn*, the First and Second Destruction (of the Temple)." Born in 1941 in the Warsaw Ghetto, this poet is unequivocally rooted in the matrix of history. Beginning with almost total disintegrative loss—of family, community, culture, country and language—she has taken up the task of recreating herself as Jew, woman, and writer, by facing and learning to articulate that destruction. If she had stopped there, had become only the author of her early poems and of *"Bashert,"* she would be recognizably one of the most powerful poets to have addressed those events.

But Klepfisz's poetry goes further—not by way of leaving behind *der khurbn*, an impossibility for any Jew, or any non-Jew who wants to understand living in the twentieth century—but by searching, through her poetry, for what is possible in a world where *this* was possible. Her own existence itself cannot be taken for granted; what it depends on, that mixture of chances and will, is the theme of *"Bashert."** Most poets emerge with existence itself as a given (though not always with literacy as a given, literature as a given); this poet cannot:

> during the war
> germans were known
> to pick up infants
> by their feet
> swing them through the air

*Yiddish word meaning predestined, inevitable.

and smash their heads
against plaster walls.

somehow
i managed
to escape that fate.

Lines like graffiti on a wall. The consciousness that, precisely, existence itself is not to be taken for granted, will inform her further explorations.

What it means to be a Holocaust survivor or the child of survivors is a question that has haunted Jewish life since 1945: through denial and silence, through amnesia and mythologizing, through a search for resonance. Certainly in the United States it has had its own reverberations and failures of resonance. For Klepfisz this is not just a question of present meaning, but of lost, irreplaceable resources, cultural and emotional riches that were destroyed or scattered before she could know them. The question for her is, then, also what it can mean to grow up as a Jew in the United States in the years after *der khurbn*; and what it means to grow into a Jewish woman, single, childless, a lesbian, an artist, in a community of survivors who see their great hope for meaning in a new generation of Jewish children. What is allowed, what is available, to the poet thus located?

Before *der khurbn* Yiddish poetry—the tradition Klepfisz might "under other circumstances" have possessed as a continuing heritage—was a poetry largely written by men yet written in the language called *mame-loshn* or "mother tongue": vivid, emotionally vibrant, vernacular, as opposed to Hebrew, the language of scholarship and religious study, reserved to men only. Yiddish was a people's language, a women's language, the language of the Ashkenazi Jewish diaspora. The women poets of this tradition (many of whom are still untranslated, so that we have but a few names: e.g., Celia Dropkin, Anna Margolin, Kadia Molodowsky, Fradel Schtok, Malka Tussman) were known as more sexually frank than the men; but even of them the Anglophone reader knows only what's translated. It's a dead-end to try to imagine what might have become of Yiddish poetry, or of Klepfisz as a poet, in a different history. The only history is the one we know, however imperfectly: that a great Western cultural movement was exterminated, not only under the Nazis but under Stalinism. And, to the present day, many Europeans of both east and west, many Americans of both north and south, are unaware of or indifferent to this.

The great flowering of Yiddish literature took place in the late nineteenth and early twentieth centuries, along with the rise of Jewish secularism and the Jewish labor and socialist movements. It is from out of these traditions that history uprooted Irena Klepfisz, depositing her into a community of survivors in New York.

In a time when speculative biography has been replacing serious writing about poets and poetry, I touch on this poet's personal history with some reluctance, and only because it seems to me inseparable from a serious reading of her work. We have seen an obsession with intimate details, scandals, the clinical or trivializing reduction of artists' lives. The biographies of poets fetch a far higher price than their poetry. It is also true that when a poet who is not male (or white) writes from direct experience, this poetry is subsumed as mere documentary or polemicizing. If I speak here, then, of experiences from which Klepfisz's poetry has been precipitated, it's because a historical necessity has made her the kind of poet she is: neither a "universal" nor a "private" stance has been her luxury.

The ghettoes instituted by the Nazis were not equivalent to those medieval ghettoes which Jews themselves petitioned for, communities where they could try to protect themselves and each other against Crusader mobs. The ghettoes of the Nazi period were part of the plan to destroy the Jewish people in its entirety. Throughout Poland, thousands of Jews were forced to retreat into increasingly densely populated areas enclosed by walls and barbed wire. By 1940 nearly half a million Jews were locked, compressed, within the Warsaw Ghetto; by 1941, the year of Klepfisz's birth, the penalty for attempting to escape was death. Of course, they were all under sentence of death. Eighty-three thousand Jews died from hunger and disease within twenty months in the Warsaw Ghetto alone. The ghettoes were holding-pens for Jews destined for forced labor camps and ultimate destruction—bases for selective deportation.

Throughout the ghettoes Jews organized armed resistance movements. In Warsaw they constructed tunnels leading to the sewer system for escape and for bringing in arms and explosives. In street-to-street and under-street fighting the Jews held out. In April 1943 the Nazis decided to subdue the ghetto through an air attack. In this battle Michal Klepfisz, the poet's father, was killed. Because her mother had blue eyes and spoke fluent Polish, she and her infant were able to pass, and were hidden by Polish peasants. Polish became Klepfisz's first language. They emigrated after the war to Sweden, then to the United States when Klepfisz was eight years old, where she learned English in school while living in a world of spoken Yiddish: a world of people who had carried the remains of their culture to another continent, in their memories, in old snapshots and documents, archives rescued from conflagration, reconstituted institutions. And, not least, Klepfisz's mother, as a presence in her poems, embodies continuity, endurance, and the oral tradition's access to the lost.

The shattering of a culture is the shattering not only of artistic and political webs, but of the webs of family and community within which these are first nurtured and transmitted. The two long poems (unpublished till now) which open this book delineate the search for what has most intimately been lost: the father-hero-martyr whose absence becomes enormous presence:

> These two:
> widow and half-orphan
> survived and now resided
> in a three-room apartment

with an ivy-covered fire escape
which at night
clutched like a skeleton
at the child's bedroom wall....
The missing one
was surely
the most
               important
link....

And when the two crowded
into the kitchen at night
he would press himself between them
pushing, thrusting, forcing them to remember,
even though he had made his decision,
had chosen his own way...
he would press himself between them—
hero and betrayer
legend and deserter—
so when they sat down to eat
they could taste his ashes.

But the search is also for all "those whom I would have known /
had circumstances been different." *Had circumstances been different*:
a terse, matter-of-fact phrase behind which lies all the unprovable:
history reversed, or unwinding differently, the possibility of hav-
ing lived "an ordinary life," the life of "common things, gestures
and events" that Klepfisz invokes elsewhere, in her essay on the
Holocaust, Israel, and the Palestinians, "*Yom Hashoah, Yom Yerusha-
layim:* A Meditation": to have become, not the child survivor
lighting candles "for all the children / who have perished" but a
child playing with other children, in Jewish Warsaw, in the *yidishe
svive*, in a home peopled with parents, extended family, worker-
intellectuals.

But because "history stops for no one," Klepfisz has gone on to
write a poetry of uncompromising complexity, clothed in appar-

ently simple, even spare language—simple and bare as the stage of a theatre in which strict economies of means release a powerful concentrate of feeling.

There is extraordinary vitality in Klepfisz's early poems on women in the Holocaust. Images and voices rush. They floodlight a neglected dimension of the genocide: the survival strategies, the visceral responses, of women. They burn and bristle with urgency, contained within a disciplined and crafted poetics. "death camp" explodes all its possible meanings into a catharsis which, though suggested by the change of tone, the relief of the open vowels in the last four lines, can never be complete. It is a poem of death so alive that its smoke remains in our nostrils. "herr captain" and "perspectives on the second world war" likewise possess a control of tone and image which allows the wild and desperate quality of experience to be heard. In "perspectives," a "terror"—the woman hiding with her child, her hallucinating prescience of worse possibilities—is juxtaposed with a point later in time when to speak of such things would be "too impolite" in detached "conversations over brandy." These poems engage with physical and moral immediacy in ways that make them continuingly urgent. In them, Klepfisz takes the considerable risk of trying to bear witness to this part of her history without compromise and without melodrama. She succeeds because she is a poet, not only a witness.

"*Bashert*" is a poem unlike any other I can think of in American, including Jewish-American, poetry, in its delineations not only of survivor experience (in the skin of the mother "passing" as gentile with her infant daughter) but of what happens after survival: the life that seems to go on, but cannot persevere; the life that does go on, struggling with a vast alienation, in a state of "equidistance from two continents," trying to fathom her place as a Jew in the larger American gentile world, first as a student

walking home alone at midnight. The university seems an island ungrounded. Most of its surrounding streets have been emptied. On some, all

evidence of previous life removed except for occa-
sional fringes of rubbish that reveal vague outlines
that hint at things that were. On others, old build-
ings still stand, though these are hollow like caves,
once of use and then abandoned.... Everything is
waiting for the emptiness to close in on itself, for
the emptiness to be filled up, for the emptiness to
be swallowed and forgotten.

A landscape that might be some blasted Jewish ghetto of postwar
Europe, but is actually the edges of a Black ghetto surrounding an
elite American university.

I see the rubble of this unbombed landscape, see
that the city, like the rest of this alien country, is
not simply a geographic place, but a time zone,
an era in which I, by my very presence in it, am
rooted. No one simply passes through. History
keeps unfolding and demanding a response. A life
obliterated around me, of those I barely noticed.
A life unmarked, unrecorded. A silent mass mi-
gration. Relocation. Common rubble in the streets.

This is not the stereotypical, mass-marketed immigrant experi-
ence. The poem is not about finding safety, freedom, a better life in
America. It stares down the American myth that if you are just
hard-working, virtuous, motivated, tenacious enough, the dream
of freedom, security, and happiness can be realized. In its rhyth-
mic, relentless, almost choral double dedication, it invokes the
random and various shapes of death and survival. *"Bashert"*
mourns the dead and the survivor alike, defying such ideas as that
the fittest survive, or that victims "choose" their destiny. Moving
between poetry and blocks of prose, in a poem where everything
is made concrete and there are no cloudy generalities or abstract
pronouncements, Klepfisz has written one of the great "border-
land" poems—poems which emerge from the consciousness of

being of no one geography, time zone or culture; of moving inwardly as well as outwardly between continents, land-masses, eras of history, or, as Chicana poet Gloria Anzaldúa expresses it, in "a constant state of mental nepantilism, an Aztec word meaning torn *between ways.*" A consciousness which cannot be, and refuses to be, assimilated. A consciousness which tries to claim all its legacies: courage, endurance, vision, fierceness of human will, and also the underside of oppression, the distortions quarantine and violent deracination inflict on the heart. When I say that "*Bashert*" is a poem unlike any other I mean this through and through: in its form, in its verse and prose rhythms, in its insistence on memory without idealization, its refusal to let go.

And yet, as the poetry of this continent becomes increasingly poetry written by the displaced, by American Indians torn between the cities and the reservations, by African-Americans, Caribbean-Americans, by the children of the U.S. internment camps for Japanese-Americans in World War II, by the children of Angel Island, by Mexican-Americans and Chicanos with roots on both sides of the border, by political exiles from Latin America, "*Bashert*" takes its place (as does Klepfisz's poetry as a whole) in a multicultural literature of discontinuity, migration and difference. Much of this new literary flowering is of course, also lesbian and feminist.

The new literature of discontinuity, migration, and difference invents its poetics out of a mixture of traditions and styles, out of the struggle to name what has been unnameable in the dominant European traditions. (Yiddish itself has been disparaged by the privileging of Hebrew on the one hand and English on the other.) It is often a bilingual poetry, incorporating languages other than English, and patois, not in allusion to Western high culture, as in Modernist poetics of the twenties and after but because bilingualism is both created by the experience of being migrant, immigrant, displaced, and expressive of the divisions as well as the resources of difference. Klepfisz's bilingual poems do not—and this is significant—drop Yiddish phrases in a cosy evocation of an idealized past, embodied in *bobe* and *zayde*, or as a kind of Jewish seasoning

21

on an American tongue. Poems such as *"Di rayze aheym*/The journey home," *"Etlekhe verter oyf mame-loshn*/A few words in the mother tongue," or "Fradel Schtok" painfully explore the world of a writer located not only between landscapes, but between languages; the words of the mother tongue are handled and savored with extreme delicacy, as precious yet also tenuous legacy. In "Fradel Schtok" we enter the mind of a poet trying to change languages, far more internally rupturing than the change of countries. We meet Fradel Schtok at the moment when she feels her native language fading. *"Di rayze aheym,"* in deceptively simple and brief phrases, transposes *How shall I sing the Lord's song in a strange land?* that ancient Jewish lament, into *How shall I remember, how shall I speak, in the language of an alien culture?* There is a paradox here: Klepfisz uses the Anglo-American language with enormous sensitivity, consciousness, and art. But these qualities emerge not from a triumphant linguistic posture, but precisely from her refusal to pretend that it is the language of choice, or the supremely expressive language.

In white North America, poetry has been set apart from the practical arts, from political meaning, and also from "entertainment" and the accumulation of wealth—thus, pushed to the margins of life. Klepfisz, the inheritor of both a European Jewish Socialist-Bundist political tradition, and a Yiddish cultural tradition, naturally refuses such "enclosures." The enclosure of art in a separate sphere from daily life and work is a pressing concern for her. And surely the Holocaust itself—as well as the tradition of *yidishkayt*—demands a renewed vision of what art—poetry in this instance—stands for and against. Theodor Adorno's drastic statement that "After Auschwitz, to write a poem is barbaric," has to be severely parsed. If taken at face value it would mean a further desolation even than we have already had to face. Adorno, a German Jew who lived for many years as a refugee in the United States, may have forgotten the ancient role of poetry in keeping memory and community alive. On the other hand, his remark might be pondered by all writers who too easily find language for what they have not yet absorbed; who see human suffering as "material." Klepfisz's art resists all such temptations, both through the force and beauty of her work, and by the ways in which she demands accountability of art.

Survivorhood is not a stasis; the survivor is not an artifact, despite efforts perhaps to reify or contain her, give her the lines we think she ought to speak. These poems are the work of a woman who feels, acts and creates in living time: a feminist, a lesbian, an activist in the women's movement for many years, an essayist and editor as well as a poet.* She writes sometimes from cities where a window box, a potted plant, a zoo, an arboretum, become "mnemonic devices" for the natural world, and "water is a rare sight...but it can / be reached"; sometimes from a country-side or a shoreline where

> ...she'd never before been forced to distinguish
> herself from trees   or sand and sea.   and it became ob-
> vious that when it came to rocks   she could never prove
> her own distinctness....

From the urban plant that sensualizes the apartment where two women make love, or the fiercely generative tangle of narcissus roots in a glass jar, to a garden of wildflowers transplanted, with uneven success, to the "inhospitable soil" of a former garage, the sudden wildness of a city cat transplanted to the country, living things are charged in these poems by a fresh and totally unsentimental consciousness. There is a tough and searching empathy; the poet is not outside of nature, looking in: she is observant in both senses, participant, a different yet kindred being who instinctively responds to growth, deprivation, persistence, wildness, tameness. Perhaps nowhere is this kindredness more searingly and physically rendered than in "From the Monkey House and Other Cages," a series of monologues by female monkeys born and raised in a zoo. In this deeply original vision, the monkeys are not metaphors for women in captivity; they have a life of their

---

*A collection of her essays, *Dreams of an Insomniac*, has been published as a companion volume to this one.

own, however straitened and brutalized. Yet it's through the woman poet's eyes and language that the experience of their captivity is opened up to us.

Klepfisz is one of those rare North American artists who, within and by means of her art, explores the material conditions by which the creative impulse, which belongs to no gender, race, or class, can be realized or obstructed. "Contexts" juxtaposes the child's passion for words with the seamstress mother's recognition of how bread must be put on the table; the poet-proofreader with the aging blind scholar for whom she works; the worker going home wearily by subway with the beggar working the car. The "Work Sonnets" depict the crushing of dreamlife and imagination in those who, because of class, race, and gender, get written off by capitalism and its need for robots. But the woman clerical worker who finally speaks in the poem is not a robot; she has a dreamlife, albeit a buried one; and she has evolved her own strategies for survival, calculating closely her participation in the system, and even, ironically, in the poem. These poems are political to the core without a single hortatory line. Like their author, they do not take their existence for granted.

In a different vein, Klepfisz's poems to women lovers probe with a questioning scrutiny what happens in bed, in relationship. Sometimes, as in "periods of stress" dry humor laces vulnerability; always there is compassion for both self and other.

The last and most recent poems examine the pain and necessity of identifying as a Jew with the Palestinians under Israeli occupation. From the Warsaw Ghetto resistance to the *intifada*, the trajectory of the book is clear:

> All of us part. You move off in a separate
> direction. The rest of us return
> to the other Jerusalem. It is night.
> I still hear your voice. It is in the air
> now   with everything else   except sharper
> clearer.   I think of your relatives
> your uncles and aunts   I see the familiar

battered suitcases   cartons with strings
stuffed pillowcases
children sitting on people's shoulders
children running to keep up....

    If I forget thee
Oh Jerusalem Jerusalem Hebron
Ramallah Nablus Qattana...
    ...may I forget
my own past my pain
the depth of my sorrows.

Throughout, and in its very last lines, this book asks fundamental questions about the uses of history. That it does so from a rootedness in Jewish history, an unassimilated location, is one part of its strength. But history alone doesn't confer this strength; the poet's continuing labor with Jewish meaning does. The other part, of course, is the integrity of its poetics. A Klepfisz poem lives amid complex tensions, even when its texture may appear transparent. There is a voice, sometimes voices, in these poems which can often best be heard by reading aloud. Her sense of phrase, of line, of the shift of tone, is almost flawless. But perfection is not what Irena Klepfisz is after. It is the tension among so many forces: language, speechlessness, memory, politics, irony, compassion, hunger for what is lost, hunger for a justice still to be made, that makes this poetry crucial to the new unfoldings of history that we begin, in 1990, to imagine.

Adrienne Rich

EARLY WORK
(1971)

Searching for My Father's Body

Searching for my father's body
I begin with the index
hoping to see the name
and to catch sight of a familiar grave.

It all depends on who you knew,
or rather who knew of you,
that determines history;
which circle self-conscious
wanted to commit to paper
its existence and mark a common grave.

The shock of not finding his name
is always the same. Unused to his
anonymity, I close the books angry
that his body was not discovered
and remains buried in an unmarked grave.

It is more painful
when there is no index.
I put it off, thinking
there's time, he's been

buried for twenty-eight years;
one more day won't make a difference.

I numb myself and begin the body check
skimming quickly unwilling to be caught
in strangers' tragedies, only looking directly
at those whom I would have known
had circumstances been different.

The search leaves me weak.
I am still not hardened.
Often caught by a particular sight
I begin to read, despite myself,
and learn a new name, another event,
still another atrocity. I smell again
the burning bodies, see the flames,
wade through sewers in a last desperate effort,
till some present distraction,
like hunger or cold, draws
me back and I begin closing windows
and preparing dinner.

After dinner I procrastinate.
Again I ask myself: should I really do this

and if I do it, will it finally

be done with? Once having found him,

will I be able to leave him in his grave

or will I still insist on carrying

him with me, a thirty-year-old man

who I never knew?

Will I finally purge myself of the last image

he presented to his friends

when he chose deliberately, in split-

second consciousness, his own style of dying?

> *In one of the attics we are suddenly surrounded. Nearby*
> *in the same attic, are the Germans and it is impossible*
> *to reach the stairs. In the dark corners of the attic we*
> *cannot even see one another. We do not notice Sewek*
> *Dunski and Junghajzer who crawl up the stairs from*
> *below, reach the attic, get behind the Germans, and*
> *throw a grenade. We do not even pause to consider how*
> *it happens that Michał Klepfisz jumps straight onto the*
> *German machine pistol firing from behind the chimney.*
> *We only see the cleared path. After the Germans have*
> *been thrown out, several hours later, we find Michał's*
> *body perforated like a sieve from two machine-pistol*
> *series.*[1]

Confusing details, difficult to follow,

but the main fact, his death,

stares at me from the faded page,

stares at me without penetrating

my reason or understanding.

Simply a fact, dead,

like the object it describes.

I am dissatisfied. I am angry.

I would have liked more life

in this description.

I would have liked those present

to have stopped *(We do not even pause)*,

to have examined the body,

to have made sure no pulse was there

(We only see the cleared path),

to have described his stillness, their certainty

that he was really dead at that moment,

that they hadn't deserted him,

that he didn't lie there alone

feeling his own death.

I want more details

to fill up my emptiness.

> But the fighting had only begun. On Shwentoyerska Street
> it raged around the brush factories. A group under the
> command of Michel Klepfisz [sic] took a heavy toll of
> Germans. They battled for every building and for every floor
> of every building. They fought along the stairways until

they were forced to the top floors. Then the Germans usually set fire to the building. Our fighters would dash through prepared openings in the attic walls to begin the fight again in the adjoining building.

On the fifth day [sic] of battle, in executing such a withdrawal, Michel's group found themselves caught in an attic with German soldiers. In the dark, the fighting was confused. A German machine gun held Michel's men at bay by sweeping their side of the attic from behind a chimney.

Two comrades managed to get close enough to the main body of Nazis to throw a hand grenade. At that precise moment, Michel hurled himself on the machine gun. It stopped firing.

An hour later, when the Germans were cleared out, his comrades found Michel's body with two neat rows of bullet holes across the stomach.[2]

I do not want this death.

Instead I leap towards life

when my father

slept

Michał himself, thanks to a Polish acquaintance and worker and the two Pepesowske sisters (Marysha Sawicka and Anna Michalska) whom he had drawn into the work to help Jewish underground fighters, was able to find places where he could stay overnight, and when all doors were hermetically sealed and it was impossible to find a roof over his head, he would go to sleep in the cemetery among the graves.[3]

in Christian cemeteries,

perhaps even in the one

where his sister,

who succumbed in a hospital,

lay buried

under a Christian name.

And my father

sleeps among the graves

in Christian cemeteries

grateful

that there is a dry spell,

that the contact will have a pistol,

that he will be able to jump the wall,

that perhaps tomorrow Marysha

will find him a real place to sleep.

It is here I see him most clearly

as he sleeps leaning against a tombstone

and dreams, never considering

where he himself will one day be buried.

1. Mark Edelman, *The Ghetto Fights* translated from the Polish by Zofia Nalkowsak. (Lodz: Central Committee of the Bund, 1945).

2. Bernard Goldstein, *The Stars Bear Witness* translated from the Yiddish by Leanard Shatzkin (New York: Viking Press, 1949).

3. I. S. Hertz, *Doyres Bundistn* (Generations of Bundists) quotation cited translated by Irena Klepfisz (New York: *Undzer Tsayt Farlaq*, 1956).

The Widow and Daughter

"The widow Rose and small daughter Irena survived
and now reside in New York." Translated from the
Yiddish in *Doyres Bundistn* (Generations of Bundists).

The widow
a shadow of the wife Rose
      (he was over six feet
      and called her *Mala*,
      little one)
at one time expected
to live
      not survive.

In those days
she was romantic
      (they met one winter
      when he chased
      and overtook her on a ski slope.)
She read many novels,
knew all the love songs
      (one in particular
      was her favorite—
      ja nie jestem winna,
      it's not my fault)
knew the first part
of *Pan Tadeusz* by heart,
helped her husband
with his work
      (he was an engineer
      and she drew circles for him
      with a protractor)
and never believed
that he might die

(he was a champion jumper
and discus thrower)
but would be young always
in their apartment in Warsaw
(it was sometimes called
she told me proudly
the little Paris of Eastern Europe)
where she would receive her sisters,
nieces, nephews (one of the twins died)
and dreamed into a mist even grandchildren
of unborn sons and daughters
and looked forward to intellectual discussions
about the progress of the workers' movement,
the latest romance in a novel or the family.

Instead she survived
motherhood
(she was in labor for three days,
then he said: something has to be done)
the Aryan side
(she became a maid
and was polishing silver for *them*
while the ghetto burned)
widowhood
(as a child I asked
if she cried a lot
when they told her
and she said
yes)
and finally New York
(she became a dressmaker
and did alterations)
with the little daughter
product of three days of labor
a moving monument

whose melted existence
formed an eternal flame
(at memorial meetings
she lit candles
for all the children
who had perished).

These two:
widow and half-orphan
survived and now resided
in a three-room apartment
with an ivy-covered fire escape
which at night
clutched like a skeleton
at the child's bedroom wall.

To this apartment
which chained them
welded them
in a fatal embrace
the missing one
returned at night.

The missing one
was surely
the most
          important
link.

He held out on the fire escape
refusing to give up
his strategic position.
He was there
on the wall
with his whole family

staring out of the picture,
on the piano
staring out of the picture,
in the living room
(vying with her mother for attention)
staring out of the picture,
till the apartment
seemed to burst with his eyes
which penetrated every corner
seizing every movement of their mouths
and made them conscious
that he understood
every word they spoke.

And when the two crowded
into the kitchen at night
he would press himself between them
pushing, thrusting, forcing them to remember,
even though he had made his decision,
had chosen his own way
rather than listening to the pleas of her silence
       (she once said: I never complained about his activities
       and Michał said he was glad I was not like other wives
       who wanted to draw their husbands back into safety)
he would press himself between them—
hero and betrayer
legend and deserter—
so when they sat down to eat
they could taste his ashes.

from PERIODS OF STRESS
(1975)

during the war
germans were known
to pick up infants
by their feet
swing them through the air
and smash their heads
against plaster walls.

somehow
i managed
to escape that fate.

p o w's

the p o w's   came   home   some after
seven years   a long time   to return to
a wife   suddenly reaching   her menopause
a daughter   menstruating   every month
it's a hard lesson   to understand:
wrinkled thighs   and sagging breasts

my father came home   to me   for the first time
in twenty-nine years   just last night   in a
dream   he was old   and tired
and so scarred   so very unlike   the image
i have of him   he pulled his hat   down
over his eyes   ashamed   of his years   his shabbiness
and waited   on the staircase   hoping   i'd say
welcome home   dad
                          he was thirty   killed
by a german   machine gun   defending   the roof
of a brush factory   was declared   a hero
awarded   the highest medal   a soldier could
get awarded   posthumously
                          i am now   almost thirty-
two   should have borne   him a grandson   to carry
his name   he came home   a bit   early

herr captain

i whispered as he came   through the gate
captain   i am clean   i've been trained
well   i said   captain   i'm not over
used

he was hard   so hard   forcing bending me
till i could not breathe   slamming against me
my mouth filled with terror   i was pierced
in two   when he suddenly pulled out
my head back   he murmured   what a light rider
my grandmother   too   rode her cossack lover
in pain he moaned   harder quicker   ride me now
fearful   i ran   jumping the gate   with the guards
laughing   grimacing   through the window   nervous
biting their nails   the dogs barked   my legs spread   slapped
around his waist   i whipped him further   deeper   till
i felt the blood flooding the field   filling the drowning well
lapping over me   drinking in the smell of his hair
his stomach swollen against me   he collapsed
but i held on   pushing my heels into his back
my teeth clenched   i hissed for my grandmother   her crooked wig
her gold teeth   and her cossack lover   crawling from the well she
pushed up her buttocks as she came over the wall fell to the ground
head   first her wig cocked over one eye a butcher knife under her
skirt my mother floats in well water zeyde in mourning tears his red
hair hears them again on the kitchen floor slipping in so smoothly she
was wet from the beginning the horse neighing outside and bobe her
earspierced at the age of three weeks pulls out the butcher knife
begins slashing till his hands severed he falls back

he brings me soap
his boots are shiny
not like the others   who arrive from the fields
crusted over

In my early teens I read *House of Dolls*, a novel written by a man under the pseudonym Katzetnik 134633 and based on a diary of an anonymous Jewish woman who did not survive the Holocaust. When I rediscovered it, I immediately recognized it as the main unconscious source for "herr captain." Although today, I see sexuality and violence from a different perspective than I did in the early 1970s when I wrote it, "herr captain" is to me still an important poem about Jewish women's experience and survival.

death camp

when they took us   to the shower   i saw
the rebitsin   her sagging breasts   sparse
pubic hairs   i knew   and remembered
the old rebe   and turned   my eyes away
i could still hear   her advice   a woman
with a husband   a scholar

when they turned   on the gas   i smelled
it   first   coming at me   pressed myself
hard to the wall   crying   rebitsin   rebitsin
i am here with you   and the advice you gave me
i screamed   into the wall   as the blood burst from
my lungs   cracking   her nails in women's flesh   i watched
her capsize   beneath me   my blood in her mouth   i screamed

when they dragged my body   into the oven   i burned
slowly at first   i could smell my own flesh   and could
hear   them grunt   with the weight of the rebitsin
and they flung   her on top   of me   and i could smell
her hair burning   against my stomach

when i pressed through   the chimney
it was sunny   and clear   my smoke
was distinct   i rose quiet   left her
beneath

about my father

—he became a teetotaler out of his socialist convictions; during
        the war he began to drink again

—he was casual; he kept his tie in his pocket till the last minute
        before oral exams

—he left me on the street to be picked up by the the nuns from the
        orphanage; he watched me from a distant doorway

—once he refused to hit me; he told my mother his hand was
        too large

—he wrote to his aunt that he hoped the baby would be a boy

—when he was a student, jews were not permitted to sit in the
        front rows of lecture halls; he made it a point to
        stand through the lectures; ultimately, jews were
        allowed to sit

—he was a discus thrower

—according to some, he got along with everyone: jews, goyim,
        children

—he was caught a couple of times by the germans; they thought
        he was a polish smuggler

—once he was put on a train for treblinka; he jumped, was shot at
        and wounded, but got back to warsaw alive

—he believed in resistance

perspectives on the second world war

i

              it is a terror
in the closet   her knees
are limp   eyes straining to see
every object glows with a
private halo   pulling down
her skirt   the trickle
of urine along her thigh and calf
she wipes it carelessly with her hand
biting her lips she fixates on
pebbles and rusty nails along
the path to the truck   it is an oblivion
seen in matter-of-fact gestures
wiping the child's nose with her fingers
she says   blow   his eyes shine   as she
feels the pressure of the doorknob   palms
wet slipping out of her grasp   she whispers
not now   not yet   we've been so careful
he's a good child   just a little more time
she pleads with them   we will not be
careless anymore   this time the knob falls
into the glare of lights   voices scream
orders she does not understand   but obeys
blow   she tells him pulling down her skirt
and wiping his nose with her fingers   later
it is still over   has been over
since the knob slipped from her hand
like the wet fish that jumped while she tried
to scale it   later after the not yet
not now   the walk nude across the yard
she glimpses the meaning of the order
allows her eyes to widen for one

moment and see the path   it is a coldness
never before felt or imagined   she clutches
her hands tearing at her thighs   wailing
to the others she tries to lean on them
to explain the mistake   the small error
nothing is irrevocable   she screams   nothing
to them trying to lean   they push her away
and her hands cup the knob   for a better hold
to keep out the light   her world is cement
stone   iron

ii

listening to conversations   over brandy
i am always amazed at their certainty
about the past   how it could have been
different   could have been   turned around
with what ease   they transport themselves
to another time/place   taking the comfort
confidence of an after dinner drink

            it would be too impolite
of me to say   my mother hid with me
for two years among ignorant peasants   who
would have turned us in   almost at once   had
they known who we were   who would have watched
with glee while we were carted off   even though
grandad had bounced me on his knees and fed me
from his own spoon   and my mother is a frightened
woman

            it would be too impolite
to say   you do not know yourselves   you do not know
others

conditions

   i will take you   with me
next week   only if: you're
relaxed   and easy   and if:
you don't make   any trouble

if: you make any   and i mean   any
kind of trouble   i will leave you
here   with the two cats   a bowl
of water   and some   cookies

and i will be having   good times
without you   free without you
having nice times   not wishing
you were there   hanging on

and if: you choose to come
along   but spoil   my good times
and do not smile   and laugh
when it's appropriate

i will come   back without you
leave you there   among strangers
while i return   to the cats
and continue to feed them   regularly

and i will not acknowledge   any
postcards   telegrams   i will only say
you are out   or address unknown
or   you could be anywhere   by now

so let me repeat   and i do not make
idle threats   if: you want to stick
with me   and if: you want to go   and
want to come   with me   back and forth
smoothly   easily   you can   if: you do every
thing exactly   precisely   as i want

periods of stress

it is unwise during periods of stress
or change to formulate new theories
case in point: when about to begin
a new love affair   without having ended
the previous one   do not maintain
that more freedom is required for the full expression
of individual personality   or that various
life styles are possible   and all kinds of interesting
situations   still need to be explored.

try instead: i am tired   tired
of the nearness   this small apartment
of the watering can and level of the window
shade.   i prefer to drift towards more spacious rooms
towards intimate restaurants and dimly lit unfamiliar
beds   new love techniques.   but
do not throw me out.   i am too
frightened to venture out alone.
let me stay till i'm secure again
somewhere else   and then leave me alone.

please don't touch me

please don't touch me
wait a moment
just wait one moment
until i'm not so cold

> the spider
> with its eyes
> into my insides
> the third eye
> warm with summer
> full of light
> now shrivelled
> atrophied
> dead to light

please don't touch me
wait a moment
just wait one moment
until i'm not so cold

> the spider
> with its eyes
> awake with me
> spread out
> behind my head
> silent still
> crawling away
> with the light

please don't touch me
wait a moment
just wait one moment
until i'm not so cold

       the cracks
       ceiling torn
       caves of hollow
       if breath is strong
       silent still
       motionless
       breathless
       airless
       lightless
       silent still
       the balance
       in control

please don't touch me
just wait a moment
just wait one moment
until i'm not so cold

dinosaurs and larger issues

for rachel

i

1. & 2.   the first two nights
she lay   diagonally across
the bed   clutching at the blankets
she refused me   room & warmth

3.   the third night
she told me   i can't handle
this   i can't handle   it
i slept   in the living room

4.   the fourth night
she said   this has to be
the last night   & moved
close to me

5.   the fifth night
she did not speak   about
it.

ii

they're never as big as i imagine
rachel informs me   whenever i enter
the reptile house   expecting cobras
to be jammed   wedged   bursting out of
into   every corner of the cage   muscles
tensing   i am always disappointed

with their slenderness   their comfort
and ease   as they relax   draping casually
over plastic trees

whales   she is earnest   should
be as big as ocean liners   instead
they swim content   in aquariums
trained to jump and leap   and it's true
they're large   but not like
they're supposed to be

rachel's eyes   narrow and widen
i do not reveal   some dinosaurs
full grown   were no bigger
than hens   that she could have
roasted   and served them
for dinner   with no fear of
leftovers

iii

in the dark   her features
are distinct   her skin white
translucent.   i see outlines
of bones.   she is crystal
my fingers   feel the thinness
of the flesh.   her mouth
is hard   demanding.   she
keeps her head turned away.
she does not look   directly
at me   except to brush away
the hair from my face   before
her tongue penetrates my mouth.
then her eyes close quickly.

i study the hand's gesture
try to give it meaning.

in the dark   her features
are strong.   she lies relaxed
ready to accept   the touch
of my tongue   ready to be cupped
sucked into me   later she says
i cannot reciprocate.

iv

no i don't enjoy this
she says   biting my hand.
her mouth   which holds
endless kisses   will never
say yes to me   just the hand
across my back   like a heavy hammer
or a quick furtive kiss
on the back of my neck
tell me   perhaps   yes.

i just don't like cunts
she says   i don't like
them   she says to me.

v

i am sorry if i've made
you unhappy   i told her
sitting   at the furthest end
of the couch
                    don't make
yourself so important

she answered   with confidence
there are larger issues
at stake.

vi

it's not the kind of person
you are   i try to explain to her
you have the power   to lift
your hand   to touch me as i pass
or to walk towards me   and hold
my face   so it's not the kind
of person   you are

vii

at night   the vestiges
of other ages   influence
us.   there are
the sucking sounds   of your mouth
with mine   the moans of an ancient language
i easily recognize   my tongue
urging you on   slowly   deep
beneath the sea   or in some secret
cave   our nails: clawed   we hold
each other   you and i
released from an unexpected
danger.   exhausted we lick
each other's wounds   inflict
new ones   sharply.   our voices
echo   through the cave
return   and clash   on hard rock.

we know our bodies   and do not mind
them/ourselves   losing all sense
of proportions   limits.   we are equal
here   you and i.

afterwards   in the fire's flames
we see   cumbersome dinosaurs
rubbing their necks   against
each other   making small   sweet noises
tame and huge   so much larger than we dared imagine.

when the heart fails

when the heart fails   and over
fills with disappointment   rake
leaves   in the backyard;

gather them   in large green bags
stamp down   to make more room
gather more   and keep from the wind;

tie carefully with wire   to prevent
spillage   and going over the same ground;
since burning is forbidden   load up the car.

at the landfill   the gulls mill
and gawk   waiting.   this trip
will not please them.   there is nothing to eat.

it was good

for sharon

it was good:
the plant by your bed
green with sunlight
while we made love   your face
melted into marble
delicate pink   liquid
with desire   and later
walking through
haphazard streets
the sky empty
my arm through yours
the shrubbery   holding back
its spring greenness   your despondency
the cruising police
the slits in the blinds
the striped sun across
your face   the plant
the wetness of your mouth

flesh is cold

flesh is cold   and the bitch
moves too much in bed   crossing
and recrossing   unable to make
a warm spot and hold it   her skin
curls with the cold   shrivels
reduces her face to straight lines.
i wonder at the angle
of her back   solid in my face
she moves again   pretending
i am not there   till i pin her down
screaming   i am here   and you are not
here   alone

they're always curious

they're always curious about what you eat as if you were
some strange breed still unclassified by darwin & whether
you cook every night & wouldn't it be easier for you to
buy frozen dinners but i am quick to point out that my intra-
venous tubing has been taken out & they back up saying *i*
could never just cook for one person but i tell them it's
the same exactly the same as for two except half

but more they're curious about what you do when the urge
is on & if you use a coke bottle or some psychedelic dildo
or electric vibrator or just the good old finger or whole
hand & do you mannipppppulllaaatttte yourself into a clit
orgasm or just kind of keep digging away at yourself & if
you mind it & when you have affairs doesn't it hurt when it's
over & it certainly must be lonely to go back to the old finger

& they always cluck over the amount of space you require
& certainly the extra bedroom seems unnecessary & i try to
explain that i like to move around & that i get antsy when
i have the urge so that it's nice to have an extra place
to go when you're lonely & after all it seems small compen-
sation for using the good old finger & they're surprised be-
cause they never thought of it that way & it does seem reason-
able come to think of it

& they kind of probe about your future & if you have a will or
why you bother to accumulate all that stuff or what you plan
to do with your old age & aren't you scared about being put
away somewhere or found on your bathroom floor dead after
your downstairs neighbor has smelled you out but then of course
you don't have the worry of who goes first though of course

you know couples live longer for they have something to live for & i try to explain i live for myself even when in love but it's a hard concept to explain when you feel lonely

they did not build wings for them

they did not build wings for them
the unmarried aunts;   instead they
crammed them into old maids' rooms
or placed them as nannies with
the younger children;   mostly they
ate in the kitchen, but sometimes
were permitted to dine with the family
for which they were grateful and
smiled graciously as the food was passed.
they would eat slowly never filling
their plates and their hearts would
sink at the evening's end when it was
time to retreat into an upstairs corner.

but there were some who did not smile
who never wished to be grafted on
the bursting houses.   these few remained
indifferent to the family gatherings
preferring the aloneness of their small rooms
which they decorated with odd objects
found on long walks.   they collected
bird feathers and skulls unafraid to clean
them to whiteness;   stones which resembled
humped bears or the more common tiger and
wolf;   dried leaves whose brilliant colors
never faded;   pieces of wood still covered
with fresh moss and earth which retained
their moisture and continued flourishing.
these they placed by their dresser mirrors
in arrangements reminiscent of secret rites
or hung over delicate watercolors of unruly

trees whose branches were about to snap
with the wind.

it happened sometimes that among these
one would venture even further.   periodically
would be heard vague tales of a woman
withdrawn and inaccessible suddenly disappearing
one autumn night leaving her room bare
of herself.   women gossiped about a man.
but eventually word would come back
she had moved north to the ocean and lived
alone.   she was still collecting
but now her house was filled with crab
and lobster shells;   discolored claws
which looked like grinning south american
parrots trapped in fish nets decorated
the walls;   skulls of unidentifiable
creatures were arranged in geometric patterns
and soft reeds in tall green bottles
lined the window sills.   one room
in the back with totally bare walls
was a workshop.   here she sorted colored
shells and pasted them on wooden boards
in the shape of common flowers.   these she sold
without sentiment.

such a one might also disappear inland.
rumor would claim she had traveled in
men's clothing.   two years later it would
be reported she had settled in the woods
on some cleared land.   she ran a small farm
mainly for supplying herself with food
and wore strangely patched dresses and shawls
of oddly matched materials.   but aloneness

was her real distinction.   the house was neat
and the pantry full.   seascapes and pastoral
scenes hung on the walls.   the garden was
well kept and the flower beds clearly defined
by color: red   yellow   blue.   in the woods
five miles from the house she had an orchard.
here she secretly grafted and crossed varieties
creating singular fruit of shades and scents
never thought possible.   her experiments rarely
failed   and each spring she waited eagerly to see
what new forms would hang from the trees.
here the world was a passionate place and she
would visit it at night baring her breasts
to the moon.

the fish

for esther hyneman

directionless   it scavenged
never mapping   its own territory
or claiming   feeding rights.
it produced   spawning unfeelingly
generations unaware of their origins
remaining indifferent   to them/it   all life
except   as it provided food   in dark shadows.

there was no pattern   but
the broad cycle   and that also seemed
hidden from its consciousness   the irrevocable
past   present   future   so it was taken
by surprise   when suddenly it began to weaken
as the dryness entered its mouth   for it too
did not want to die   alone.

it lies half   eaten   brown burnt
covered in part by sand   the mouth
agonized   almost accusatory
it would be inhuman   to disturb its pain
washed inland   it sinks and drowns.

in between

it is always then
you notice   your lack
of brilliance   grace

feeling like a dying star
in the ram's horn
the fish's eye

that readies for a mute
explosion   noticed only
when its dark absence

startles a distracted astronomer.

the house

i

arranging it is far easier
than living it.   the books
stand ready on the shelves.

classifications by time or place
come naturally to me.   alone
finding the book important is difficult.

i've started to live here many mornings
opening my eyes vowing *this* morning
i will really begin.   objects intrude themselves:

floors need sweeping and one carton
unopened   is hidden in a closet.

ii

the telescope is still
disassembled   (at night
the skies are clear).

mirrors and lenses
lie in velvet lined cases.
i am afraid to use them.

iii

one of my cats was badly
clawed.   i could see layers
of muscle and fat.   my neighbor
warns there are foxes here.

i do not tell my neighbor
his cats look wild.   i do not
know my neighbor's name.

iv

there are fears to which
i do not admit.   there are fears
which i refuse to name.   alone

in the dark   i am
afraid of others   but also
of the clean smell

of the refrigerator;
the freshness of chlorine
draws me.   i walk quickly
towards the bedroom.

v

this morning   i cleaned
the yard.   i saw a face
from the city   in the trees.

the face was a mask
and i pulled it off
but there was nothing.

vi

patterns in rocks originated from
pressure.   the veins were once separate
stones   pushed together   stamped into
other hard flesh.   they merged
and became ornamental.

                              the colors
blend surprisingly well.   rings
match shapes and textures.   unwilling
inanimate   they played their roles
the iceberg scraping off layers   till
the desired smoothness was achieved.

vii

i do not understand my place
in it.   it seems to have a life
of its own   made by others
simply on loan   for a year.

they ask me: how is
your book?   and i give accurate
gas meter readings   wondering
where i will be next year.

the world here is fluid
the beaches undefined.   there are rocks
whose function   i do not know.

edges

1/

the only reason she was not able to make it on her own
though she'd been on her own and alone most of her life
was that she'd never before been forced to distinguish
herself from trees   or sand and sea.   and it became ob-
vious that when it came to rocks   she could never prove
her own distinctness.   the realization   occurring one
very clear   transparent day   when she could see all the
way to the end of the point   frightened her so much   she
ran back to the house and rolled herself up in a blanket.
first   she closed the bedroom door.

2/

the preoccupation with plants   constant watering and hover-
ing over them   checking the buds and fingering the leaves
was another major symptom.   she did not want to admit it
to herself immediately.   she continued watching them some-
times stealthily   hoping she would catch even the minutest
movement.   (she turned the plants away from the sun   and
they turned back.)   it was impossible to catch   to seize
their breath.   she would pretend that when she watered them
the leaves trembled.   but that was fantasy.

3/

though she did not want to mouth it   she knew the words
were missing.   somewhere she'd lost the vocabulary   per-
haps the black night when she pushed herself outside and
down the road   though her hands continued gesticulating
when she ran towards the ocean.   it was a loss she did
not regret   finding it was better to listen   than to manu-
facture.

4/

she could not tell if this was birth or death   moving
out of   or into the grave.   the sand was alternately
hot and dry   and cold and wet   too extreme in either
case   and the ocean took on a different feeling each day
without warning.   in the winter the dune shrubbery seemed
to hold its breath.   she watched it keenly   her eyes
lowered   away from the horizon.

5/

she had kept the seedlings in the bedroom   but that had
become a terrible burden.   she found it impossible to
concentrate and so moved them into the kitchen.   the bed-
room door would remain closed at all times   day or night.
she lived alone   but feared intrusions she could not arti-
culate.   it was not human contact   or human harm.   ra-
ther it was   the kitchen   its smell of food which frightened
her.   it was undefined   and she desperately needed strict
outlines   an unfilled space demarcated.   she chose the bed-
room   keeping the door closed   day and night.

6/

whenever the phone rang she was startled   not because she
didn't expect anyone to call   but because it seemed that here
surrounded by sand   and smell of salt and cooking meat   the
ring was inappropriate.   it was as if some strange creature
had made a demanding noise   insisted on recognition which she
was unwilling to give.   she never knew how to speak   or what
to say.

7/

crushing time between waking and sleeping was a daily con-
cern.   she moved slowly hoping it would move past   post-
poning the waking moment till almost stupor.   it was all
limitless.   seeing the beach fade into the fog   she'd
turn suddenly and discover her footprints had already been
covered by the wind.   no trace at all   as if she'd been
born on that spot in that moment.   she was amazed how
easily markings disappeared and became a part of the shore.
the bluffs stood coldly   eroding.

8/

there had been that moment looking down toward the point
when the horizon had distinctly separated the ocean and sky
and waves came in regular motions   building and collapsing
in unending fury   that she felt herself losing ground   eva-
porating.   she tried to think of the small pale blue flower
which had appeared the day before.   but it was drowned in
the foam which ran towards her toes like soapsuds.   the
water receded   taking the flower with it   and she watched
as she was pushed inland   and the wet sand was pulled away
from her until she felt in one moment it would be too late
and ran back to the house   and rolled herself up in a blank-
et.

9/

the pale blue flower was a surprise.   the plant seemed to
be only leaves.   she had stared at it for a long time try-
ing to remember a word   brack   or bracti   she could not re-
call exactly a lesson she'd once heard.   she was frighten-
ed again.   all this breath   she thought.   she considered
withholding water   that was for a fraction of a second   and
then watered it immediately.   supper had to be cooked.
she checked the bedroom door.

10/

she knew of course that here it would have to be serious
because no one would look in or call   for days   so it was
a serious decision to be weighed carefully   and when fully
sober.   she continued collecting rocks   arranging them on
the deck   planting new seeds   and feeling the scratching
as imperceptible as a forgotten dream   down at the base of
her skull.   she continued cooking   and freezing the food
and answering the phone when it rang   and trying to remember
old words she once knew: viscera   stasis   inchoate.

11/

there was no saving here and no one to advise her and she
really did not want to listen except whether it was acidic
or alkaline   and whether sun was necessary   or humidity   or
if repotting might be helpful for growth   or if fertilizer
had to be used.   she kept taking books out of the library
renewing them   but it was hard to hold it all in.

it culminated in a rage she could not contain.   the door had
not been closed properly   and was pushed open by the draft
from the kitchen   the curtains moved as if breathing in and
out against the screen.   she knew it was too late   and she
could not control it anymore.   she walked to the beach and
scooped up the foam rubbing it against her face.   she squeezed
slimy seaweed   till it squirted strange juices   that trickled
down her legs like green semen.   she walked for a mile collect-
ing all the fish skulls she could find   and arranged them in
concentric circles   placing a rock in the middle.   finally
she carried some large stones to the foot of a bluff   hoping
to prevent erosion.

riverhead: a center

i

　　　　　　　　it is a training
　　　　center.　　　　children learn
　　　　to sit still　　　to keep
　　　　fingers out of mouths
　　　　to point to their noses
　　　　socks　　　to clap hands
　　sit still　sit on the toilet
　　to bite sandwiches　to keep
　　fingers out of mouths　to
　　flush the toilet　　to drink
from a cup　　to point
to hair knees　　to sit on command
to sit still
　　　sit still
　　　　　　sit still.

　　　　　　i have come here
　　　to see myself
　　　as i glimpsed my image
　　　one summer　to forget
　　　your stone eyes
　　　my inadequacy in them:
　　　as you turned the page
　　　and completed the sentence
　so vital　flicking me away.
　these of some other age
　half formed　crepuscular
　creatures　who never recognize
　the sun　touch me deeply

In Riverhead, New York, there is a training center for retarded and disabled children.

allow me to return to
myself again.　　away from
your marmoreal pose　　the spastic
gesture
　　　springs life.

ii

　　　it is too much
this pressing against.
　　　　i can't push my words
　　　　into your ears　　nor force
　　　　words out of your mouth
nor carve your lifeless
　　　　figure　　into an action pose.
　　　　i see you move　　from place
　　　　to place:　　you are at work
now at home　　　　turning
　　　　the page of a book.　all
　　　　patterned　　set in a motion
　　　　which defies disturbance.
you guard your mechanism
　　　　carefully:　you say　　these
　　　　are private things and i won't
　　　　discuss them.　there is
no touching you　　though you
　　　　vowed　your eyes big
　　　　moving your head
　　　　back and forth you would
never never　　let me go.

　　　　each day is a constant
　　　　repetition of memory and
　　　　gesture:　a persistency
　　　　　　which appalls　　the same

facial grimaces   twisted postures
fluttering fingers and high pitched
ooooooo.   the schedule is pinned
                to the wall: free play
bathrooming   attendance   gym
bathrooming   table work   lunch
bathrooming   resting   gym
                and each day   the puzzles
are distributed   sandwiches broken.
always the moment of self-
assertion: refusal to eat   or move
                followed by a hard slap or disgrace
behind the door   till tears come
and the lunch is thrown in the trash.
the same theme   the same applause
                repeated without boredom
pressed into them so they will not
forget.   and every day they arrive
        fresh   unaware of yesterday
its monotony.

iii

                my mother registered
                me in school.   i
        cried   holding on to her
        leg   screaming i did not want
        to go.   already wise
i knew the breach   had been completed
                but it was a scene
                i had to play.

                    i rage
                    then calmly enunciate
              my activities in a tone
              revealing: productive.
              it is a hollow anger
              and you   so impassive
                    so arched within
                    yourself   are content
      to sink into the couch   even deeper
                    into the purple velvet
                    to cover your eyes and ears
                    and mouth   you are content
        having speeched prettily of love
        of friendship   having fulfilled
        the requirements of sound   never
        your head moving back and forth
        never   to let me go   now focus
                    on the vital sentence
                    and turn the page.

                    one of the boys
                    handsome and neat
              is a perfect mimic of sounds
              and words   but he will never
              never talk.   he goes for
              religious training
                    sometimes he crosses
                    himself.

the supervisor
points to one of the girls
        (she was patterned
for many years   hours and hours
        neighbors arrived
moving her legs and hands according
        to schedule   her brain
never developed   but who knows what
        she would have been
had they let her alone):   if
        we could just
get her to walk with her head
        higher and to stop
drooling   people wouldn't be so
        repelled;   now any
one knows what she is.   the supervisor
        has straight grey
bangs and smiles her easy concern:
        the disgusting habits
must be concentrated on   must be
        eliminated.

            i have
        never kept the right public
image for you   and privately i've been too demanding
        too volatile   spreading myself
out across your room   insisting intimate knowledge of
        each corner.   but i've seen your face
chalk with sudden fear   your eyes widen with pain.   i've
        seen you lose control
in the gesture of a hand   a turning away to stare
        at a picture on the wall.
we manipulate every moment   refusing to acknowledge
        what we feel.   i am too

crude   and you not crude enough   stubbornly silent
        at critical moments   when one
word would have eased me.   we no longer like
        each other.   we've become
            unsuited.

v

            the place is an armory:
its garage a gymnasium;   off to one side
is a stockroom;   the walls are lined with
            fresh smelling pine clubs
which hang gracefully from clean leather straps;
the metal shelves are filled with blank eyed
            gas masks;   a vault-like closet
contains ammunition.   at the end of the day
the children gather for gym.   some ride tricycles
            some stare blankly at the walls.
any noise from them   is always a relief to hear.
the superintendent of the building   pats them
            on the head as he passes.
occasionally a young soldier stops and says something;
but usually he is embarrassed or visibly repelled
            by their strangeness.

            last night i dreamt
        we met and embraced whispering forgiveness
for past cruelties.   you held my hand
            i kissed your hair.
        this morning i felt relieved.   i knew it
was finally completed.   i would stop trying
            to deny the breach.
        we would finish in silence   masked again
unfamiliar   with our very mouths   hands
            our very veins.

aesthetic distance

only it
can help in the arrangement

: a child   fat
ordinary   except
for its flabbiness
                  except
for the bullet hole
through its belly

: a discolored puncture

: a mother (or grandmother
leathered   hard
staring
beyond the bullet hole
beyond the belly

into a dry   brown
hard part of this earth

self-dialogues

i

it seems that you and i
have not talked
now   for a long time
and today   walking by
the gardens   i first noticed
how trees have their own
diseases   cancerous-
like growths that choke
their trunks.

                    once
when i saw a tree cut in half
i said in surprise
it is wet
and you said back:
it is a living thing
and we tend to forget
that like blood
this transparent
dew   leaks life.

i'd forgotten your existence
your heavy boredom in winter
the wetness of life   sitting
here   staring at the incomplete
dry wooden bookshelves   waiting
to be trimmed   sanded
smoothed down from original irregularities
how trees have their own

diseases   that wound
and suffocate with sawdust
their rigid arteries.

ii

today   the day
had no beginning
in the afternoon
i took a walk on the esplanade
and stared at the river.

water is a rare sight
in the city.   you have to search
for it   through secret sidestreets
of elegant neighborhoods
or abandoned factory areas
with punctured windows.   glass
remains a deterrent.
                        but it can
be reached   and from a certain
height   retains a quality
of purity freshness   though
perhaps it is too tame
too calm today   to reflect its
ocean origins.

iii

it is not a question
of belonging   but rather
of finding a place
and you   are difficult
to place.

the decor of the apartment
has been set   i've worked
hard for the final effect
the position of planters
the colors of the prints
the wall rugs   a feeling
of easy life   with the darker
tones of understanding.

                    frankly
i don't want to disturb
the current scheme   and it is
inconvenient   to say the least
of you to come now   at this time
when i had it all so well arranged
insisting   with your monotony
on the pain.

                    yes yes
pain is a part of life
but i'd prefer
you kept yours
to yourself.

iv

i've recognized you
in the terror-worn
faces of old women
pigeon feeders   who
carry frayed social security
checks   and politely belch
their acid-eaten stomachs
behind their hands.

i've seen you
in the words
of their forced conversations
with young cashier girls
all pink in their
striped uniforms
young girls
who smile   pity
in embarrassment.

i remember how you
used to stand
putting on lipstick.
they also preen
and watch the color run in the cracks
of their skin   and
smear into a wound.
how coquettishly
they prepare
for street society
for passers-by   pulling
down their skirts
over their tired bodies

saying: well someone
will see   and it is always good
to look nice.

i've never liked looking
at them   though i've
stared in pained fascination
thinking of you.

v

i would never have placed
you here   but rather in
some cardboard room   a meager
supply of food in the refrigerator.

and yet i've been lonely
of late   and would not mind
some company   just to fill up
the space.   the living room
is lovely this afternoon
light with sun;
some plants are already
beginning to bloom   and
perhaps it might cheer you
to take in the warmth   of the colors
here

i would not mind
such company
that drank in the brightness
and felt my efforts
nourishing.

vi

last night i dreamt i was
a gaunt   and lifeless tree
and you climbed into me to nest.
you were calm   so serious
as you wrapped your legs
around my trunk   and pressed
your body against me.   and
wherever your human skin
touched my rough bark   i
sprouted branches   till
lush with leaves   i grew
all green and silver   frail
like tinsel   holding you
asleep   in my wooden arms.

Two Sisters
(1978)

THE TWO SISTERS WERE BORN IN HAMBURG, GERMANY; HELEN IN 1933 AND Eva in 1936. In 1938, their parents placed them on a children's train to Holland, to safety, to an aunt and uncle who never came to pick them up in Amsterdam. So the girls were sent to a Catholic children's home, safe in Holland, Catholic, out of Germany. But Eva became sick, was taken to a hospital, alone away from Helen, and Helen stayed in the home with the rest of the children, alone away from Eva. After a few months, their parents arrived and the Hesse family was reunited.

In 1939, the Hesses emigrated to safety, to the United States. During the next few years, their parents separated, divorced, found other partners. The girls lived with their father and his new wife (whose name was also Eva), went to school. Six years after their arrival, their natural mother sought safety again, committed suicide in 1945. From then on, her daughter Eva feared January.

The two sisters grew up, got married. Eva was an artist, became known, got a divorce. Her father became ill, had to be watched and cared for for many years. He died in 1966. And then Eva became sick, went to the hospital, found she had a brain tumor, cancer. She died at the age of thirty-three. This was in 1970.

The following is a monologue by Helen Hesse, surviving older sister of the artist Eva Hesse and sole surviving member of the Hesse family.

Two Sisters: A Monologue

I.

Her nightmares were always worse
though I remember more of what
actually happened: the nuns polite
indifferent   the marble floors
my knees   white with numbness
from kneeling too long.
She dreamt of black pockets of space
starless voids through which she'd float alone
nothing to touch   nothing to be touched by.
Then she'd wake   and scream into the night
and Papa would come   to tighten the covers.
He'd whisper: "You're perfectly safe now.
Hush.   I've tied you down."

Her screams would
cut off my dreams   of the good-bye kiss
the brush of skin
against skin
in heavy damp air
how Mamma wiped tears from her dark deep eyes
then straightened the fur piece   around her collar
and   how Papa pinned our names to our coats
telling us softly: "Be strong, be proud."
And then   I'd watch them again and again
standing and waving   their handkerchiefs high
till they were so small   just bits of mud
on the splattered glass.

II.

There are times   when the heart
like a young   and inexperienced
ancient queen   sick   and over-
burdened by nightly dreams   begins
to harden   to close in upon herself;
nor does she find ease   or safety
in the words of the sorcerers
astronomers   in the scheming court.
Instead   determined   she watches
learns in silence   that all times
are times of crises
that throughout her lifetime
there will be no peace
that again   and again   her realm
will be besieged by warring tribes
with alien   unpredictable ways.
And so   she tightens the borders
around her unhappy realm   and rules.

                    The heart   too
when unprepared for the world and its rude ways
mistakenly learns   to exclude pain and pleasure
alike   hoping to achieve serenity.

III.

Take, for example, the children:
She simply did not understand   about them
that they were not pieces
whose internal wiring   could be bent
and twisted out of an unnamed need
or discarded when they resisted imagined forms.

They were not art.
Whenever she'd visit   she'd sit and watch
as hand in hand   they'd choreograph
maneuvers   on their blazing boards
bend with the curves of the hill
like birds I've seen   perhaps imagined.
She'd look astonished   and she'd laugh:
"You've forged the great American dream."
Then she'd turn and think about something else.

In Europe   life was less distinct:
more room—no—a tendency towards shadows
within the ancient   stone yards.
The beggars   begged among the poor
calling to the shuttered windows
their monotonous   call.
It was—not a gloom exactly—
but an earnestness   a realization
of the seriousness of things.   And Eva,
she, I think, felt safer with those day time shadows
more at ease with light   transformed and stretched
by osbtructing walls   into a narrowing darkness.

It was quite simple: I preferred the sun.

IV.

Europe was history and sepia: photographs frayed
at the edges   sometimes torn or folded
thick postcards   slashed   the face scarred
the body stiff and awkward.   With luck
you'd see the eyes   wide
a sense of life   of attitude: the cap
in hand   slicked down hair   buttoned shoes.

But always   they remained   an earthly brown
and with age   the light around them brightened
and the figures would bow   into a faded background.

Our albums   are so different
harsh with colors   seen
only   on clear and sunny days
on empty beaches
water reflecting light   of sun and sky
are such colors   ever seen.   Yet in our albums
they glow   in every season   in any place
bright and sharp   such health and freshness
in the midst   of foul urban air
or war   or sickness: such health and freshness
in our photographs.

V.

She'd never leave   old wounds alone.
I'd   reason with her   to get more control
but she'd press her lips   and say: "Let's face it
we're just not the same."   And turn her back
as if— it's hard to say what she really wanted.

Once, I remember she said to me:
"You're like a fortress
I once dreamed of: all mortar   stone
and iron.   I scaled its walls   with bare
hands and feet   tearing myself on the crude
exterior.   Eventually   I reached the top
gained access to its rooms and halls.
Inside: it was quite empty.   Helen   it
protected nothing."
                        She had a way
of hurting deeply   then pulling back.

She'd begin to cry
then touch me   with such ease
hold my face   between her hands.
She'd sob and weep
in a rush of ecstatic love:
"Helen, forgive me.   You know how I am."

I've never felt that free.

VI.

I'd sometimes visit her in New York
and stare across the river at the Jersey shore.
I'd try to see it   through her eyes.
"Dead," she'd say   without a second thought.

Her art was everything.
She never understood   that I needed
ground   a place to root myself
to tie myself down
that I could not float   like she did
never knowing what strange   new thing
would burst from me   demanding of attention.
She'd cry: "You're lucky, you've escaped
the terrors."   I'd bite hard and reply:
"I've fought to keep them out."

VII.

I read statistics about this place.
Yet I feel safe.   The children are strong.
He's always with me.   I'm not alone.
Perhaps that's weak.   I still think
she did not have to be   the way she was.

I've survived   just by my own will.
She died of illness.   Yet the critics are sure:
she wouldn't have lived longer   anyway.
Young death is suicide   no matter what.

But I see her so clearly.
I remember   one day   how she turned   bewildered
frightened   already ill.
"Helen," she said, "I've just begun
to understand it all.   Why now?   Is it my fault?
Must it end badly   botched up   like it began?"

Sometimes at night I circle the room
like an angry tiger around its prey:
genes   environment   our own will.
But I'm no expert on these things.
Resistance's elusive.   The children complain
that I am too hard.
I feel jealous of him   when one of them cries.
But I'm afraid   I want them to know
how easily these battles   are lost.
I want them to know—
and then I think:

      Eva, sister—what dreams we both had.

from KEEPER OF ACCOUNTS
(1982)

for Judy Waterman

I

*From the Monkey House and
Other Cages*

From the Monkey House and Other Cages

The voices are those of female monkeys born and raised in a zoo.

Monkey I

/1/

from the beginning
she was always dry   though
she'd press me close
prying open my lips:

the water warm
the fruit   sour   brown
apples bruised and soft.

hungry for dark   i'd sit
and wait   devour dreams
of plain sun and sky
large leaves   trunks   dark
and wet with sweet thick sap.

              but morning
brought back the space
and cement   her weakened
body   my head against her
breast: my mouth empty.

/2/

yet she was   all
my comfort: her sharp
ribs against my cheek
her bony fingers   rough
in fluffing me dry.

she showed me   all
the space   the changing
colors outside   then

pulled me back   forced
me to sit with her
in a shadowy corner.

on certain clear days
she'd shrug   hold me in the sun:
her fur lacked smoothness
her body warmth.

/3/

in the midst of heat
they took me   with smooth
round strokes   and hushing
sounds.
              she sat silent
at first   sniffing their sweat
their stale breath   then leaped on one
her eyes wide   her claws poised and sharp.
              he grunted   deep
from within   an empty cavern
echoing the storm outside
flicked her off   and dragged me out.

i could hear her sound
as if a sea lion roared
then becoming tired
                        drowned.

/4/

their space was smaller
cramped and low   the air
foul   with their sweat
their salt.
            and their motions
were sharp   as they spread me out
clamped me down
for the opening probe.

            i did not move
just sucked my breath
with each new venture   into my deepest parts
and then   with time
i became   a dark dull color
a gray rain   blending
with the liquid   of her eyes.

/5/

when they returned me
the air was ice:
bare branches   meshed
against a hard   dark sky.

i sat alone.   we were
separate now   though
she was still there
in the cage   next to mine.
her fur was stiff   her nostrils spread
she eyed me   circled
her back arched   ready for attack.

later   as the food was dropped
she leaped forward
hissed   snatched bits of fruit
from my side   of the bars.

/6/

a day   and a day
the pools   dead and dry
i'd sit and stare
into the cold   into the empty trees.

but she seemed   at rest
pressing against the bars
eyes closed   alone   on the other side.
only when i ate   she'd look sharp at me
her mouth moving
as i swallowed   each bite

and as night blackened us
she'd gather her scraps
enclose herself   in her arms.

/7/

the male   sleek-furred
was young   and active
when they forced him through to me.

i stayed in place   all
eyes and ready   while she leaped
in frenzy   retreated to the furthest wall.
he kept his distance
ignoring her   ignoring me
ate small morsels   tumbled
stared outside.

the ice was thawing
the pools filled and quiet.
i listened   as the soil
sopped   became mud
deep   and brown.

/8/

soon the trees budded   and i
pinked   softened   and presented.
he penetrated   withdrew
penetrated   withdrew
over   and over
till i was dry
and hard.
          she sat
relaxed and quiet
began to chew apples
slowly picking out
each black seed.

/9/

                    later
i cramped   shrivelled
then opened   wide   wide
my flesh thin and stretched
till: it burst forth
a thing   so strange
so pale   and hairless
a mass of flesh   separate from mine.

and through the heat
and heavy trees   the sound of water
the light of the moving sun:
the male ate regularly
the small one sucked
i mashed the sour fruit
between my lips.

she watched us all
as we would swallow
hoard   any piece of rind
or seed   that she could find.

/10/

the male was taken:
i turned my back.
the small one was taken:
i was held to one side.

and again   and again
the trees emptied again
the soil became hard
then became soft again.

and the cage is   all
mine   and i have myself:
touching my fur
pulling my face

while she moves so slowly
without any sound
eating   pacing
twisting her arms   around the hard bars.

/11/

sometimes at night   i watch
her asleep: the rigid bones
the thinned out fur

and i can see clearly
the sky   the bars
as we sat together
in a spot of sun
and she   eyes closed
moved me
moved me
to the sound of the waters
lapping
in the small   stone pools
outside.

Monkey II

/1/

to state each horror
would be redundant.   the objects
themselves suffice: a broken comb
an umbrella handle   a piece of blue
plastic   chipped pocket mirror.

the face is unfriendly.
i try to outstare it   but
it persists   moving

spastically   the eyes
twitching   open   shut
nose quivering   wrinkled fingers
picking at the ears.   i do not know

this stranger.

/2/

i have heard of tortures
yet remain
strangely safe.

          but at night
i am torn by my own
dreams   see myself live
the grossest indignities   probes

and unable to rip myself from my flesh
i remain silent   not
uttering sound   nor moan   not
bothering to feel pain.

waking   in early light
alone   untouched
i cry over my safety.

/3/

when they first come
they screech with wildness
flinging themselves against the wall
and then against the bars.

some sit and cry for days
some   never recover and
die.
        they are familiar
yet crap uncontrollably   plead
shiver and rock.   i refuse

to have anything to do with them
till they learn to behave.

/4/

at her arrival   she was
stunned and bruised.   she
folded up   refusing to eat

her mouth grim.   i staked
out my territory   recognizing
her fierceness   her strength.

but she weakened   grew sick
was removed without resistance
returned three days later
shaved patches on her arms.

later she told me: we create
the responses around us.

/5/

i remember the grasp of her claws
the vicious bite   the scar
still on my leg.   she was crazed

jabbering   then attacking
again.   and the sun seemed to fall away
into coldness   as i pressed myself
against the corner   the hardened sand
under my nails.   i began to gnaw
through concrete   my face raw.

they took her away
and when she came back
she did not look at me.

/6/

scatter yourself
i told her   moving
myself into the left
corner   where i sat
observing the movement
of her head.

         she nodded
seemed to sleep
then stood up   pointing
outside.   the leaves were
red.   it was a falling time
noisy   dry twigs cracking
off nearby trees.   i felt

content   watching myself
while she pointed   the leaves
red.

                        and finally
she said   this is enough
and began to bang her head
against the wall   one thud

after another thud   she batted
herself beginning to bleed
throwing herself and falling.

they came   and tried to seize
her   while the sun vanished
and the trees   moved slowly

and everyone   so still
afraid to breathe: the moon
all fresh   and the birds
small balls of feathers.

i puked as they dragged her out:
tufts of fur on the stone floor.

/8/

when she died   i mourned
a silent mourning.
                    and
the others asked
asked   asked
and poked at me.

there had been much between us
in gesture.   mostly i remember
her yellowed teeth   her attempt
at tameness.

/9/

there had been no sound:
just the motion of   our hands
our lips sucked in
toes pointed   outward.
it had been enough.

                    dizzy
with messages   i would lie
down   dream of different
enclosures.

II

Different Enclosures

Contexts

for Tillie Olsen

"Dollars damn me."
            —Herman Melville

"I have no patience with this dreadful idea that whatever
you have in you has to come out, that you can't suppress
true talent. People can be destroyed; they can be bent,
distorted, and completely crippled."
            —Katherine Anne Porter

I.

I am helping proofread the history
of a dead language. I read out loud
to an old man whose eyes have failed
him. He no longer sees the difference
between a period or a comma, a dash
or a hyphen, and needs me for I under-
stand how important these distinctions are.

The room is crammed with books, books
he had systematically tagged for future
projects—now lost. Sounds pour out
of me. I try to inject some feeling
and focus, concentrate on the meaning
of each linguistic phrase. On the edge
of my vision, he huddles over a blurred
page, moves his magnifying glass from line
to line, and we progress. Time passes.
My voice is a stranger's, sensible and
calm, and I, the cornered, attentive hostess,
listen in silence as it conjectures the his-
tory of languages long dead without a trace.
How, I wonder, did I become what I am not?

I request a break. The sounds cease.
I check the clock, calculate, write
figures in a notebook. I am numb
and stiff, walk up and down the hall,
stare into busy offices. I wait.
I wait for something forgotten, something
caught and bruised: a brown feather,
a shaft of green light, a certain word.
I bend, drink water, remember stubborn
clams clinging to the muddy bottom.

II.

The building across the street
has an ordinary facade, a view of the park
and rows of symmetrical spotless windows.
Each morning, the working women come to perform
their duties. They are in starched white,
could pass for vigilant nurses keeping
order and quiet around those about to die.
And each morning, idle women
in pale blue housecoats, frilled and fluffed
at the edges, stare out of double windows,
waiting for something to begin.

With whom would you change places, I ask
myself, the maid or the mistress?

III.

The clock sucks me back. I calculate the loss,
return to the books, his unrecognizing eyes.
He is unaware of the pantomime outside,
feels no rage that I and the world are lost
to him, only mourns the words dead on the page.
We begin again. I point to the paragraph,
synchronize the movement of eye and mouth,
abandon all pretense of feeling. Silently I float
out, out toward the horizon, out toward the open sea,
leaving behind the dull drone of an efficient machine.

                                        I am
there again, standing by the railing, watching
the whales in their narrow aquarium, watching
their gleaming grace in the monotonous circle, watching
how they hunger for fleshly contact, how the young keeper
places his human hand in their rough pink mouths,
rubs their tongues, splashes them like babies. I cannot
watch them enough, but feel deeply ashamed for I know
the price.

With a shock I realize we are not together,
that he is lost, caught in a trap.
He sounds the words over and over, moves
the glass back and forth, insists there is
a lapse in meaning. I sit silent, tense, watch
as he painfully untangles the subtle error, watch
as he leans back exhausted saying: "I knew something
was wrong! I knew from the context that something
was wrong!"

IV.

At the end of the day I stack the galleys,
mark an *x* where we've been forced to stop.
He is reluctant to let me go, anxious, un-
certain about the coming days, but I smile,
assure him they'll be all the same. Alone,
I rush for the bulb-lit train, for the empty
corner of the dingy car, then begin the struggle
against his vacant stare, against the memory
of the crowded shelves.

It is a story, I tell myself, at least
a story, that one Sunday when I refused
to go to work. Fifteen, bored with inventory
and weekend jobs, I stayed in bed and,
already expert, called in sick. Her rage
was almost savage, wild. She paced
through the apartment, returned to me again
and again saying *"Get up! Get up now!"*
as if I were in mortal danger. But nothing
would move me from my bed, from the sun
cutting through the iron fire escape outside,
from the half-finished book about the man
and the whale. "It's not that much money,"
I called to her.

And then her inexplicable silence. At first
she sat in the kitchen, fingering the piece
of cloth, staring absently at the teacup.
Finally she got up, began pinning the pattern.
Soon I heard the clean sound of the scissor
against the kitchen table, then silence again
as she basted. Much later that day, she worked

on the machine, and still she did not speak
to me, just let the bobbing needle make its own
uninterrupted noise. And as I went to bed
new with the excitement of that sea of words,
filled with my own infinite possibilities, she
continued sewing, fulfilling her obligation
for the next day's fitting.

V.

The blind man balances easily in the rocking
car. He moves among us, sings, shakes a tin
cup. Most of us think it's all a con, but it
makes no difference. Pose is part of necessity.
Riding each evening through the echoing tunnels,
I've begun to believe in the existence of my own
soul, its frailty, its ability to grow narrow,
small. I've begun to understand what it means
to be born mute, to be born without hope of speech.

Work Sonnets
with Notes and a Monologue about a Dialogue

I: Work Sonnets

i.

iceberg
I dream   yearning
to be fluid.
through how many nights
must it float   cumbersome
for how many centuries
of sun   how many
thousands of years
must it wait
so that one morning
I'll wake
as water of lake
of ocean
of the drinking well?

and day breaks.

ii.

today was another day. first i typed some
letters that had to get out. then i spent
hours xeroxing page after page after page
till it seemed that i was part of the machine
or that it was a living thing like me. its
blinking lights   its opening mouth   looked
as if they belonged to some kind of terrible
unthinking beast to whom i would always be bound.
oblivious to my existence   it simply waited
for its due   waited for me to keep it going
waited for me to provide page after page after page.
when it overheated   i had to stop while it
readied itself to receive again. so i typed
some letters that had to get out. and he said

he was pleased with the way things were going.

iii.

today was my day for feeling bitter. the xerox
broke down completely   and the receptionist
put her foot down   and made it clear to the repairmen
that *we* couldn't afford to keep such a machine
and it was costing *us* extra money every time *we* had
to xerox outside. they hemmed and hawed and said
the fuzz from the carpet clogged things up   and
then they worked on it. and she watched over them
and made sure it was going properly when they left.
by then i'd fallen behind and he asked me to stay
late   and i said i was tired and really wanted to go
home. so he said it was really important and i could
come in late tomorrow with pay. so i said okay and
stayed. but i didn't feel any better about it.

a morning is not an evening.

iv.

volcano
I dream   yearning
to explode.
for how many centuries
of earth   relentless
grinding   how many
thousands of unchanged
years   buried
will it take
so that one morning
I'll wake as unfettered flame
as liquid rock
as fertile ash?

and day breaks.

v.

today was my day for taking things in stride.
i was helpful to the temp in the office next
door   who seemed bewildered and who had definitely
lied about her skills. the dictaphone was
a mystery to her and she did not know how to use
the self-erasing IBM nor the special squeezer
to squeeze in words. she was the artist type:
hair all over the place   and dirty fingernails.
i explained everything to her   during her coffee
break   when she had deep creases in her forehead.
i felt on top of things. during lunch
i went out and walked around window shopping
feeling nice in the afternoon sun. and then
i returned and crashed through a whole bunch

of letters so i wouldn't have to stay late.

vi.

today was my day for feeling envy. i envied
every person who did not have to do what i
had to do. i envied every person who was rich
or even had 25 cents more than me   or worked
even one hour less. i envied every person who
had a different job   even though i didn't want
any of them either. i envied poor homeless children
wandering the streets because they were little
and didn't know the difference   or so i told myself.
and i envied the receptionist who'd been there
for years and years and years and is going to retire
soon   her hearing impaired from the headpiece she'd
once been forced to wear. for her it was over.
she was getting out. i envied her so much today.

i wanted to be old.

vii.

rock
I dream   yearning
to yield.
how many centuries
of water pounding
for how many thousands
of years   will it take
to erode this hardness
so that one morning
I'll wake
as soil
as moist clay
as pleasure sand
along the ocean's edge?

and day breaks.

viii.

today we had a party. he said he had gotten a
new title and brought in a bottle of wine during
lunch and we all sat around and joked about how
we'd become such important people and drank the
wine. and the receptionist got a little giddy
and they told her to watch it or she would develop
a terrible reputation which was not appropriate for
someone her age and maturity. and she laughed and
said "that's all right. i'll risk it." and the temp
from the office next door came in to ask me to go to
lunch. so we gave her some wine and she said she'd
been hired permanently and was real happy because
she'd been strung out and getting pretty desperate.
i noticed her hair was tied back and her nails neater.

and then we all got high and he said to everyone
this was a hell of a place. and then he announced
he had a surprise for me. he said he was going to
get a new xerox because it was a waste of my time to
be doing that kind of work and he had more important
things for me to do. and everyone applauded and the
receptionist said she hoped this one was better than
the last because we sure were losing money on that
old clinker. and he assured her it was. and then he
welcomed the temp to the floor and said "welcome aboard."
and he told her across the hall they treat their people
like we treat our people and their place is one hell
of a place to work in as she'd soon discover. and then
he winked over in my direction and said: "ask her.

she knows all about it."

ix.

dust
I dream   yearning
to form.
through how much emptiness
must it speed
for how many centuries
of aimless orbits
how many thousands
of light years   must it wait
so that one morning
I'll wake
as cratered moon
as sea-drenched planet
as exploding sun?

and day breaks.

and day breaks.

II: Notes

Says she's been doing this for 12 years. Her fifth job since she started working at 18. The others were: office of paper box manufacturing company (cold and damp almost all year round); office of dress factory (was told she could also model for buyers; quit because buyers wanted to feel the materials and her; was refused a reference); real estate office; and this, which she considers the best one. Through high school, she worked part time contributing towards household expenses.

Extremely sharp with them. Says: "I'm not a tape recorder. Go through that list again." Or: "It's impossible. I've got too much to do." Two days ago, she told me: "Make *them* set the priorities. Don't make yourself nuts. You're not a machine."

Am surprised, because I always feel intimidated. But she seems instinctively to understand power struggles. Is able to walk the fine line between doing her job well and not knocking herself out beyond what she thinks she is being paid for. And she *is* good. Quick. Extremely accurate. Am always embarrassed when they return things with errors and ask me to do them over again. Never happens to her. She's almost always letter perfect.

I've told her she should demand more. The dictaphone is old and the typewriter is always breaking down. She should make them get her better equipment. It's too frustrating the way it is. She shrugged. Said it really didn't matter to her. Was surprised at her indifference.

Friendly, yet somehow distant. Sometimes I think she's suspicious of me, though I've tried to play down my background. I've said to her: "What's the difference? We're doing exactly the same work, aren't we?" Did not respond. Yet, whenever I've had trouble, she's always been ready to help.

Her inner life: an enigma. Have no idea what preoccupies her. Would be interested in knowing her dreams. Hard for me to imagine. This is a real problem. First person demands such inside knowledge, seems really risky. Am unclear what the overall view would be. What kind of vision presented. How she sees the world. How she sees herself in it. It seems all so limited, so narrow. Third person opens it up. But it would be too distanced, I think. I want to be inside her. Make the reader feel what she feels. A real dilemma. I feel so outside.

Says she reads, but is never specific what. Likes music, dancing. Smokes. Parties a lot, I think, for she seems tired in the morning and frequently says she did not get much sleep. Lives by herself. Thinks she should get married, but somehow can't bring herself to do it. "I like having the place to myself," she said the other day. Didn't specify what she was protecting.

Attitude towards them remains also unformulated. Never theorizes or distances herself from her experience. She simply responds to the immediate situation. Won't hear of organizing which she considers irrelevant (and also foreign inspired). Yet she's very, very fair and helpful to others and always indignant if someone is being treated unfairly. Whenever a temp arrives, she always shows her what's what. Tells her not to knock herself out. Reminds her to take her coffee break. Once gave up her lunch hour so one of them could go to the dentist for a bad tooth. Did it without hesitation. For a stranger.

Q: Is she unique or representative? The final piece: an individual voice? or a collective one?

I've learned a lot here, I think. It hasn't been as much of a loss as I expected. At least I've gotten some ideas and some material. But thank god I'm leaving next week. Can't imagine spending a whole life doing this.

III: A Monologue about a Dialogue

And she kept saying: "There's more. Believe me, there's more."

And I was kind of surprised because I couldn't imagine what more there could be. And then I began to wonder what she meant by the more, like maybe a bigger apartment or more expensive restaurants.

But she said that wasn't it, not really. "I'm not materialistic," she said and then looked kind of hopeless, as if I could never understand her. "I just want to *do* something," she said, obviously frustrated. And she looked hopeless again. And then she took a big breath, as if she was going to make a real effort at explaining it to me.

"It's just," she said, "it makes no difference whether I'm here or not. *Anyone* can do this. And I've always wanted to do special, important work."

Well, that made me laugh, because I've stopped wanting to do any work at all. All work is bullshit. Everyone knows that. No matter how may telephones and extensions, no matter how many secretaries, no matter how many names in the rolodex. It's all bullshit.

But she disagreed. "No," she said. "There's really important work to be done."

"Like what?" I asked curious, for I've seen enough of these types running around telling me how important it is to do this or that and just because they're telling me it's important they start feeling that they're important and doing important work. So I was curious to see what she'd come up with.

But she was kind of vague, and said something about telling the truth and saying things other people refused to say. And I confess I'd never heard it put that way before.

"I want to be able to say things, to use words," she explained.

"Oh, a writer," I said. I suddenly understood.

"Well, yes. But not like you think. Not romances or anything like that. I want to write about you and how you work and how it should be better for you."

"So that's it," I said, understanding now even more than I had realized at first. "So that's the important work. That certainly sounds good. Good for you, that is. But what about me? Do you think there's more for me? Because I'm not about to become a writer. And I don't know why I should just keep doing this so you have something to write about that's important. So can you think of something more for me? I mean I can't do anything except this."

And I could feel myself getting really mad because I remembered how in school they kept saying: "Stop daydreaming and concentrate!" And they said that your fingertips had to memorize the letters so that it would feel as if they were part of the machine. And at first it seemed so strange, because everything was pulling me away, away from the machine. And I really wanted to think about what was going on outside. There seemed so many things, though I can't recall them now. But they kept pushing me and pushing me: "Stop daydreaming! Concentrate!" And finally I did. And after a while it didn't seem so hard to do. And I won first prize in class. And the teacher said I'd have a real good choice in the jobs I could get because quality is always appreciated in this world and with quality you can get by.

And when I remembered how I'd sat doing those exercises, making my fingertips memorize the letters, I was real mad because she was no different than the others. There's always something more. More for them. But not one notion about something more for me. Except maybe a better machine so that I can do more work more quickly. Or maybe a couple of hours less a week. That's the most that they can ever think of for me.

And I was so furious. I'd heard all this before. And I know that as soon as they tell you they'll fight to get you better working conditions, they go home and announce: "You couldn't pay me enough to do that kind of work." That's what they say behind your back.

And I started to yell at her: "If you got words and know what to say, how come you can't come up with something more for me?"

And she was so startled. I could see it in her eyes. I mean you've got to have nerve. I'm supposed to just stay here while she writes about me and my work.

And then I said: "They're always going to need people to type the final copies. And I can see you'll never waste your time with that once you've thought of all the right words." And she kind of backed up, because I must have looked really mad. And she bumped into the file cabinet and couldn't move back any further. And I said to her: "What's the difference to me? It's all the same. I always end up doing the same thing. So let's make it clear between us. Whenever you finish whatever it is you're writing about me and my work, don't count on me to help you out in the final stages. Never count on me, no matter how good the working conditions."

A Poem for Judy
beginning a new job

I will keep this simple
not give it
universal significance
nor transform it
into art.

You say:
"I will not do this
forever. I *will* paint."

I've learned now
that it's no solace
to point out   the others
so many others
straining   wasting
unable to do
what they know
they must do

for such loss
is always solitary
and unshared
outside the scope
of bloodless theory.

You do not paint
and what must happen
does not happen:
the transformation

on the empty canvas
of the elusive marble
into the shadowy water
or of the simple water
into impenetrable rock

and nothing
nothing
not even a loving embrace
nor special intimate
midnight talk
will ever make up
or diminish
that loss
for you
or for her
or her
or her

or her.

III

Urban Flowers

Mnemonic Devices:
Brooklyn Botanic Gardens, 1981

1.

I'd forgotten. Despite the planters
blossoming in the northern light
despite the potted succulents
over which you take such care
and patience   despite the window boxes
wired to the crumbling ledges
I'd forgotten.

This morning   at the pond's edge   we watch
the energetic ducks   chase and fly
in enigmatic patterns. I declare it
a mating dance—an educated guess—
having lost the thread of cycles
seasons   time   except when April's
sharp insistent air   distracts us
from this city's bitter dream
and we rise one morning   and remember:

there are still the gardens.

2.

It is a ritual   for us
this annual return
to the unsuppressed spring
in this guarded landscape
to the flowers   and trees
earth   rocks   pond.

It is the stuff of mythology
both old and new   as we relive
once more   a certain day
suddenly grown   strange
and dim   and how we stood
uncertain and afraid
of the exploding lightning
and the silent trees.

That day   awakened in us images
long lost   amid the dangers
of the city streets   and
we stood amazed   at the sight
and sound   wondering
what else   we'd lost.

That day   the gardens
drenched in violent rains
were transformed   into a raw
uncultivated place. And we
were   wearied wanderers
dazed   in awe   having suddenly
stumbled into our native land.

Royal Pearl

Where do new varieties come from?
   General Eisenhower is a red tulip which was
first recognized in 1951.
   In 1957 a lemon yellow mutation appeared in a
field of red General Eisenhower tulips. This yel-
low mutation proved to be a stable sport which
was called—Royal Pearl.
         —Brooklyn Botanic Gardens

In dead of winter   imprisoned within
the imprisoned earth   it was a leap
defiant   of all eternal laws   and patterns.
Beneath the frozen earth   it came to be
like a splitting of an inner will
a wrenching from a designated path
a sudden burst   from a cause unknown.
And then in spring   it opened: a lemon yellow
in a pure red field.

Our words deny the simple beauty
the wild energy of the event. *Anomaly
deviant   mutant*   we're always taught
as though this world   were a finished place
and we the dull guardians   of its perfected forms.
Our lives are rooted in such words.

Yet each winter   there are some
who watch   the gardens   emptied
only white   as the snow presses
on the fenced-in grounds   just
as on an unclaimed field.
And each winter   there are some
who dream   of a splitting of an inner will
a wrenching from the designated path
who dream a purple flower   standing solitary
in a yellow field.

Lithops

Common name: living stone

Barely differentiated
from the inorganic   they conceal
their passions   in sheer survival.
It is philosophy: life's hard
growth and erosion   even rocks
in the end   are broken down
to formless dust.

But like all schema   incomplete
for between the grey and fleshy
crevices   strange blossoms grow
in brazen colors. For us it is
the ancient sign   that every life
has its secret longings   to transcend
the daily pressing need
longings   that one day   must flower.

Aesthetics

No beauty for beauty's sake here.
Life's too lean
a constant   "Let's get down
to brass tacks." Function and necessity.
Stone and water.

Like the popularity of narcissus bulbs
this season. Not as you'd expect
for the plant itself   which sprouts
endless green stalks   that rise up
stiff and straight   and then finally
eke out a few buds of puny white flowers.
Nor for the obvious lesson by example:
the unavoidable six weeks (maybe more)
of patient preparation   before
any real prospects of blooming.

But rather   for the roots beneath.
Brown tipped and firm   they probe
and press around the artificial stones
in intricate networks   even dead-end mazes
daring anyone to trace them back
to their original source. In the stores
the saleswomen warn: "They can toss
the stones right out of the container!"
And here   that remains the real attraction.

Winter Light

Almost December. Indifferent
to seasons   the marigolds
persist. I am surprised by their pluck
and lack of propriety
their ability to ignore
the inappropriate:
a rusted leaking window box
a shaky fire escape
leading to a cemented street
below. They do not mourn
that all good things must
come to an end   and accept
that end as fate or destiny.
Instead   without struggle
or assessment of soil
moisture   heat   air   they continue
blooming   in chilling winter light
exactly as they did all summer.

Oleander

A gift from a lover when things
were definitely   going downhill.
"It's poisonous," she said.
"No known antidotes."
After the breakup   long after
when I'd already settled down
with someone else   I boarded it
with my mother   who's always taught:
never throw anything out.

Whenever I see it   I am drawn again
to the sembling innocence   among the dark
green jade and purple passion. I long
to taste one leaf   one petal   to test
that warning   for nothing   I tell myself
not even death   could be that final.
You must understand   it is more
than mortal resistance
for there was a time   when she left
and I knew   was fiercely certain
this departure   was the last.

Cactus

for my mother
Rose Perczykow Klepfisz

The pot itself was half the story.
A yellow ceramic dime store knickknack
of a featureless Mexican
with a large sombrero   pushing a wagon
filled with dirt.

The cactus was the other half.
Self-effacing   it didn't demand much
which was just as well
since she had no spare time
for delicate cultivation.
Used to just the bare essentials
it stood on our kitchen windowsill
two floors above the inhospitable soil
and neither flourished   grew
nor died.

I'd catch her eyeing it
as she stood   breathless
broiling our dinner's minute steaks
her profile centered in the windowframe.
She understood   the meaning   of both pot
and plant   still would insist there was
something extra   the colors yellow
green   or as she once explained
in her stiff   night school English:
"It is always   of importance to see
the things aesthetical."

Abutilon in Bloom

for Diana Bellessi

Abutilon: flowering indoor maple; houseplant

Cultivated inside   out of the bounds
of nature   it stubborned
on the windowsill   six winters and springs
resisting water   sun   all researched care.
It would not give   beyond its leaves.

Yet today   in the morning light
the sudden color asserts itself
among the spotted green   and I
pause   before another empty day
and wonder at its wild blooming.

It leans against the sunwarm glass
its blossoms firm on the thick stems
as if its roots
absorbed the knowledge
that there is no other place
that memory is only pain
that even here   now
we must burst forth with orange flowers
with savage hues of our captivity.

IV

Inhospitable Soil

i can't go back
where i came from was
burned off the map

i'm a jew
anywhere is someone else's land

—Melanie Kaye/Kantrowitz

Glimpses of the Outside

in memory of Marcia Tillotson (1940-1981)

A place

1.

Cherry Plain was once called South Berlin   before
the war   and then they probably became self-conscious.
Many here   go back before the Revolution   are of
Hessian descent   fought with the British. They are
wary of strangers   defined as anyone who has not lived
here since birth. Still they chat politely   wave
as I drive by. The children are more open   stare
shamelessly   at the new woman in town. It is a quiet
place. One post office. One small general store.
It could have grown and developed   when they expanded
old route 22. But it would have meant   cutting into
the cemetery   and of course   that was out of the question.
Like disgruntled children   they protest over their parents'
limitations   for they see   they could have gotten something
off the weekenders   rushing back and forth on Friday
and Sunday nights. But ancestors will have their way.
So 22 looped around it   leaving the town intact   except
for the occasional stranger   who is looking for a way out.

2.

I have decided not to plant a garden   only to scavenge.
Already last year's furrows   (the result of others'
labor)   are vague   and the borders almost completely
obscured by the undisciplined   self-absorbed growth.
It is what we know of weeds: no delicate sense of

intrusion   of transgressing bounds. They move in
take over   and that's that. It doesn't bother me
this unreflecting rudeness. I am satisfied to witness
the few carrot sprigs   onions   tiny lettuce heads
and without commitment   to clear weedless islands
around them. The asparagus reaches its full growth
merges with the stalk   and goes to seed. The delicate
dill   follows suit   achieves its natural toughness.
I do not intercede   in these events.

3.

This house was once a meeting hall   then a dance
hall   a polling place. More recently   a garage.
I want to plant flowers around its edges   bring
to life an image   I have had about it. But the
earth is naturally tough with rocks   and more   it
is clogged with rusted screws and washers   sparkplugs
colored chips of glass   all conspiring against my
trowel. Then too there is the heavy oil   already
congealed   fixed and unyielding   like ancient geological
strata. The inner image long forgotten   I tense
against this human resistance   push harder towards
an earlier time   towards less polluted soil.

4.

I have started transplanting wild flowers   whose
names I do not know. Small blue ones from a lake
in a state park. They are modest   with pale yellow
centers   used to the moisture of the water's edge.
I douse them every morning to make them feel at home.
From a roadside   I dig out bright yellow ones   plant
them by the unpainted barn   so I can see them from my
window as I work. These thrive   as if their sole pur-

pose   was my pleasure. But exotic   tall purple flowers
with bulb-type roots   strong like twine in their tie
to the earth   and to their particular spot   these shrivel
up a few hours after being placed by the barn. I consider
the possibilities: individual will   personality   simple
biochemical make-up. Whatever. These do not adapt.
They stand tall   and elegant   dried by the sun   next to
the brilliant yellow flowers   for whom a place by the barn
is as good   as a roadbank.

5.

Midnight: the meadow is sparkling with fireflies.
I had always thought   that at night   they folded their
wings   over their iridescent bodies   and darkened
that light. Yet here they are   in constant motion
lighting against the shadow of the mountain. The
memory suddenly comes alive   like the underside of
a non-living stone. I am eight years old   and it is
almost dusk. The fireflies rush   through arid city
air. I trap them in a milk bottle   hoping to create
a lantern to light my way home. I do not understand
that not even the dusty grass   hurriedly pressed through
the narrow bottleneck   will keep them alive   that
inevitably   in such confinement (is it a lack of air
or simply a lack of space for flight?)   their light will
dim and die.

6.

What could go wrong in such a setting? I ask
myself   thinking of that arid air   left behind
of the wino sleeping in my doorway   every night.
This valley   is so quiet   so clear and sharp-
edged   in the summer daylight. The old houses

meticulously painted   and the lawns carefully mowed
declare only: order and plain living. What could
go wrong in such a setting? I ask myself again.
The mountains look permanent   eternal in fact
though all I read about human life   about natural
evolution   tells me everything is in constant
motion   that this landscape was once of a different
sort   that these people who distrust strangers
were once strangers themselves   that the sign
"Indian Massacre Road"   a sign indistinguishable
from any other in lettering and color   posted modestly
at an obscure crossing   is but a barely noticeable
vestige   of one history forgotten and unattended.

7.

The pump is old   its age reflected in its weight
iron   shaped and welded more than a half a century ago.
It draws the water noisily   slowly   sounding like
a failing heart   pounding against itself. The plumbers
cluck their tongues   in masculine admiration. "She's
a goddam antique"   the young one says. He is tall
and handsome   with clear blue eyes. "Don't make those
anymore"   he continues   with a voice of experience
his age denies. I suspect he's only an apprentice   for
he descends into the well   while the older man sits
casually on the ledge   occasionally offering advice.
They're in agreement   or in cahoots. Get a new pump.
This one's definitely shot. Not worth fixing   the parts
too difficult to find   and when found   too expensive.
I decide against it   at least for now   and tell them
to see if anything can be done. Later   I return and
ask   if they can patch it up. "Sure"   the young one
answers. "I'll take anything on   as long as it's white."

A visit

1.

The woman who is coming to visit   is my mother.
Her life   has been bracketed by historical events
over which she's had no control. During World War II
she developed a canniness for detecting Jews   did
not care how many documents they had to prove   who
they were not. She knew. She could tell   by a special
look in their eyes   a gesture of the hand   a confidence
too casual. This acquired ability   so finely tuned
during the war years   remains alive   so that today
decades later   she cannot wander far from her Jewish
neighborhood   before she begins assessing   who are
the safe ones   and who are not.

2.

Her survival   (and as a result mine)   was partly
dependent on: her small nose   her grey eyes. And
most critical: her impeccable Polish   (with no trace
of a Yiddish accent)   because an older sister had
insisted she attend Polish schools   to gain greater
mobility. It was one perspective on the Jewish condition
in Poland. At critical moments   these elements   heredity
and environment   combined in the right proportions to
create luck. But there was also another   character
or in this case   guts. When the Germans came for her
she begged: *Ich habe ein kleines kind.* And when she
saw   the sliver of hesitation in their eyes   she ran
and took her chances. They did not chase   or shoot
just let her go. For months   she convinced the peasants
she was a Pole   playing a part   ad-libbing the dialogue
without a flaw   pretending to be the human being   they
assumed she was. During this time   she learned survival

depends on complete distrust. Even today   she is still
fierce   in her refusal to rely on others. Some would call
it alienation. Others pride. I think   it's only
the necessary stance   of any survivor.

3.

History   she says with irony   has a way of repeating
itself. *Then*   she outwitted two German soldiers   probably
young men   taught from childhood   the hideousness of
Jews. Faced with a woman   fair and ordinary   pleading
for her sickly child who would be orphaned   they must have
thought: No   this cannot be that Jewish monster. And
she escaped. At least momentarily. *Now*   she is trapped
again. But no walls or barbed wire   around her this time.
No plans for uprisings   or secret meetings. Each evening
she returns   hurrying through the orderly streets   ominous
in their emptiness   and steps into the elevator. I want
to offer her advice   strategy   a philosophy   but know their
utter uselessness in this age. For *now*   is a vastly
different time and place. The country is not occupied
by strangers. Those she fears most   are not an enemy.
And neglect and hunger   cannot be outwitted.

4.

We visit the Hancock Shaker Village   walking through
the restored buildings   recreated workrooms and living
quarters. I note the quietness   the simplicity of
the line   and wonder about the eye that fashioned it
the aesthetic vision   the philosophy of light   air
of raising the struggle for survival   above humiliation.
We pass through the herb garden. My mother stops
looks in amazement at the round stone barn   and marvels
how all this could have come   to a dead stop   without

catastrophe   without disaster. She scrutinizes the
photographs of children   adopted and nurtured. "How
could they not have wanted children of their own?"
she asks   having always believed   that one's own blood is
the sole source   of all security. And I see her shift
as she tells me again   of the children   hidden in convents
baptized and converted   then claimed by relatives after
the war. Many were finally kidnapped   by their protectors
bribed and bought off. Some could never be reclaimed.
For those who were   it was hard   painful   but my mother
adds   "They were our only hope."

5.

But it is not simply a question of reproduction
I tell myself that night   thinking of my own child-
lessness. They lacked something   which would have
pushed them on   which would have given them   a hook
in time. But it was time itself   that they ignored
thinking the farmland and woods   around the village
the seasons emerging predictably   in full character
the day and the night   all these   they assumed were
heaven   eternal. At the end of each day   after baking
and laundry   welding and weaving   tending the children
and the fields   they would meet   and reaffirm their faith.
First they shook out the sins from their bodies   then
danced holding their palms up   to gather in the blessings.
There was no time   there was no death. And so they
lived   and so they died.

6.

My mother boards the train   and sits behind the
tinted glass. She mouths words and gestures   nothing
I can understand. I raise my arms in frustration
motion her to try again. She does   but the barriers
remain. She writes a note   on a piece of paper   holds
it against the glass. The European script is clear:
"It is empty here. It is cool." I smile   and give
the okay sign. She will be comfortable on her trip back
to the city. Still· I am all anxiety. Departures
swell old   undefined fears in me   the fear of permanent
separations. Old   long-forgotten departures   which
remain active in me   like instinct. The fear of being
lost and never found   of losing all trace   all connections
severed   the thread broken. (When after two years   she
came to get me from the orphanage   I cried when I caught
sight of her   and raised my arms to her. I was barely
three   but I had not forgotten.) Of endless   futile
searches for relatives long vanished   or even worse
alive   but not traceable.
The train begins to move. My mother sits behind the
tinted glass and waves. Her face becomes an angle   and
then disappears. Her words were: "Find a place where
you are happy." But the sound of those words   had
the mourning of separation.

A place in time

1.

The postmistress is insecure in her calculations.
She checks   and rechecks all her figures   never having
the ease of certainty. Still   I trust her view
of this place   for she has that tutored eye   able to
detect the changes   nuances and variations   whose
implications   remain obscure to my alien reasoning.
She is chatty   inquisitive. Sometimes   I think she must
be lonely   sitting all day by herself   behind the old-
fashioned post office boxes   decorated with elaborate
brass eagles. Perhaps the grocery will be sold (and then
we'll be stuck   with whoever buys it). Perhaps the mail
truck will be traded in   (and then we'll have regular
delivery). Perhaps the church will be painted   by early
fall (and we can begin having services again). Perhaps
the rumors about the metal barrels   buried in the nearby
camp grounds are true   (and we should stop swimming
in that lake).

2.

At first   the cats were cautious   flattening
themselves   along the ground   slinking close to
the edges of the house. No vestigial recollections
springing from the unconscious depth of the species.
Or so I thought. But now   and I can hardly measure
the time elapsed   they act as if it's all they've
ever known   routinely bringing in mice from the meadow
or bodies of birds   necks snapped   heads hanging
like colored limp sacks. I glimpse my favorite
the tortoise shell   eating a rabbit   whose belly seems
expertly slashed and exposed. She hunches   over it

calmly chewing   the juicy red meat   patiently breaking
through   the sinewy flesh.

3.

At the Burr & Grille in Averill Park   only men
are at the bar. They look like mechanics: oil
streaked pants   workgloves stuffed in pockets.
They swap army stories   their glimpses of the
outside. In Haiti   I overhear   there are only
the rich and the poor. "Nothing in the middle"
a man in his twenties says. The rich live on top
of the mountain   the poor by the sea. They earn
about $35 a year. "Imagine the kind of life   *that*
is. They're starving. Imagine! In this day and age!"
Burr   behind the bar   clucks his tongue. "In China"
he says   "they fight over candy bars. Imagine what
that must be like." The young one begins again:
"You know   you get off   and they have all those
bands and colorful costumes   and everything is all
welcome. And then you take five steps away from
the pier   and *wham!* [he bangs his hand down on the bar]
they're ready to slit your throat   to get that wallet!"

4.

Saturday: The Baptist Church flea market and auction
offers the predictable merchandise. Old clothes
battered pots and pans   chipped glassware   rusted lawn
furniture. "It's all for a good cause"   a woman tells
me   and mentions interior renovations. I wonder if I'm
the only Jew in the crowd. An older man approaches.
"Smile!" he orders. "The Lord loves you! Certainly
the Lord loves you!" I nod   feel uncomfortable   move
towards another table. A woman   about seven months

pregnant   is having her purchases priced. She is no
more than twenty   with a small pale face   faintly freckled
deeply worn. Dressed in colorless bermudas   and a gray
blouse   she holds a carton of baby clothes. On the ground
by her feet are cheap games of plastic   a round container
with broken wooden logs   the debris of an old erector set.
This too   is her collection   the necessary response
to life's gnawing insistence on itself   on not being
ignored. She looks wearied   almost emptied by her vigilance.
I watch as she hands over the ten dollar bill and waits
for the change   watch   as she smiles   and turns away.

5.

I ride the backroads   far from any village or town
far from the blacktops   carefully numbered. Woods
along both sides. Suddenly   I am startled by an
unexpected home   a trailer on a small patch of cleared
land. Logic would say   that it had no stability
the cinderblocks at its corners appearing flimsy   unable
to keep it firmly rooted to the ground. Yet the faded
paint   the obvious rust creeping along its outer shell
reveal a hard-won permanence. Barefoot children stop
playing in front of a torn screen door   stand anxious
tentative   waiting for the unfamiliar car to pass.
A woman's eyes   keep guard at a kitchen window. Plastic
deer and clay ducks line the worn path. Junked cars
spill out of the collapsed garage. Gray overalls   and
bright sheets with sunsets   dry between two shade trees.
In a carved out tractor tire   painted red and white   grow
yellow marigolds   blue petunias. An orderly vegetable
garden on one side   loose piles of freshly split logs
on the other   testify to the implacable needs of winter.
All is urgency   asymmetry in this territory resistant
to maps and philosophy. Only the seasons   and birth

and death   remain stark. I know   I see   I learn again
from the anxiety in that woman's eyes   in the caution
of the children's stance   that there is no escape.

Mourning

1.

I reread his letter. He writes about your struggle
Marcia   your will to survive. I read the letter again
and stare at the mountain's outline   behind the house.
It is will   against the dark shadowy mountain   that I
keep thinking about. How you refused   up to the last
moment   refused to say   it is over   but stretched out
your time   how you were willing to endure the pain   how
you would not be separated from it   because it alone
held the possibility of life. A few days before you died
a friend said: *Everything's collapsing   but she simply*
refuses. I think about that refusal to cooperate   to give
yourself an easeful death. It is your will   Marcia
I am trying to understand.

2.

Why so hard to absorb   after all the waiting?
The daily calls   and reports   turned your body
into a machine. The nurses were polite   precise.
Respiratory arrest. Cardiac failure. She's
breathing on her own now. Somewhat better.
"How is her spirit?" I ask stupidly   as if
the answer could make a bond between us. One
time they said: She is angry.   Another: She is
somewhat anxious.

3.

Death asserts itself as everywhere   pulls me out
of the eternal   roots me in this time   in this place.
Your death   Marcia. After thirteen years of struggles
who would have thought   this was the final one   who
would have thought   this one was different   from all
the others? It is something I must plant   I keep saying
as if I could contain the loss   by finding the right
piece of ground   by the barn perhaps   or by the gigantic
ash   that hovers over the house   a tree planted by
a neighbor's father   more than sixty years ago. I
need a place for your death   Marcia   for it feels like
an emptiness   that can erode   all the mountains
that protect this valley.

4.

But there is no possibility of containing it. All
the days merge   and only hindsight   reveals the subtle
but discrete changes: the shortened daylight
the slowly   yellowing grass. I place seeds in the bird
feeder   write letters home   check the final stages of
the garden's undisciplined growth. Everything is
shrivelling   emptying itself of body and substance
huddling closer and closer to the earth. I plant bulbs
like a skeptic   never fully believing   these drab
lifeless lumps   will bloom next year   in full exotic color.
Nothing   I think   staring at the sixty-year-old ash
should be taken for granted. I push my trowel   deeper
sift out the slivers of glass   the heavy nails   place
the bulbs in their designated places   then cover them
with soil   flattening the surface with my hand.

Bashert

These words are dedicated to those who died

These words are dedicated to those who died
because they had no love and felt alone in the world
because they were afraid to be alone and tried to stick it out
because they could not ask
because they were shunned
because they were sick and their bodies could not resist the
disease
because they played it safe
because they had no connections
because they had no faith
because they felt they did not belong and wanted to die

These words are dedicated to those who died
because they were loners and liked it
because they acquired friends and drew others to them
because they took risks
because they were stubborn and refused to give up
because they asked for too much

These words are dedicated to those who died
because a card was lost and a number was skipped
because a bed was denied
because a place was filled and no other place was left

These words are dedicated to those who died
because someone did not follow through
because someone was overworked and forgot
because someone left everything to God

Bashert (Yiddish)—inevitable, (pre)destined.

because someone was late
because someone did not arrive at all
because someone told them to wait and they just couldn't
any longer

These words are dedicated to those who died
because death is a punishment
because death is a reward
because death is the final rest
because death is eternal rage

These words are dedicated to those who died

Bashert

These words are dedicated to those who survived

These words are dedicated to those who survived
because their second grade teacher gave them books
because they did not draw attention to themselves and got lost
in the shuffle
because they knew someone who knew someone else who could
help them and bumped into them on a corner on a Thursday
afternoon
because they played it safe
because they were lucky

These words are dedicated to those who survived
because they knew how to cut corners
because they drew attention to themselves and always got
picked
because they took risks
because they had no principles and were hard

These words are dedicated to those who survived
because they refused to give up and defied statistics
because they had faith and trusted in God
because they expected the worst and were always prepared
because they were angry
because they could ask
because they mooched off others and saved their strength
because they endured humiliation
because they turned the other cheek
because they looked the other way

These words are dedicated to those who survived
because life is a wilderness and they were savage
because life is an awakening and they were alert
because life is a flowering and they blossomed

because life is a struggle and they struggled
because life is a gift and they were free to accept it

These words are dedicated to those who survived

Bashert

1. Poland: My mother is walking down a road.

My mother is walking down a road. Somewhere in Poland. Walking towards an unnamed town for some kind of permit. She is carrying her Aryan identity papers. She has left me with an old peasant who is willing to say she is my grandmother.

She is walking down a road. Her terror in leaving me behind, in risking the separation is swallowed now, like all other feelings. But as she walks, she pictures me waving from the dusty yard, imagines herself suddenly picked up, the identity papers challenged. And even if she were to survive that, would she ever find me later? She tastes the terror in her mouth again. She swallows.

I am over three years old, corn silk blond and blue eyed like any Polish child. There is terrible suffering among the peasants. Starvation. And like so many others, I am ill. Perhaps dying. I have bad lungs. Fever. An ugly ear infection that oozes pus. None of these symptoms are disappearing.

The night before, my mother feeds me watery soup and then sits and listens while I say my prayers to the Holy Mother, Mother of God. I ask her, just as the nuns taught me, to help us all: me, my mother, the old woman. And then catching myself, learning to use memory, I ask the Mother of God to help my father. The Polish words slip easily from my lips. My mother is satisfied. The peasant has perhaps heard and is reassured. My mother has found her to be kind, but knows that she is suspicious of strangers.

My mother is sick. Goiter. Malnutrition. Vitamin deficiencies. She has skin sores which she cannot cure. For months now she has been living in complete isolation, with no point of reference outside of herself. She has been her own sole advisor, companion, comforter. Almost everyone of her world is dead: three sisters, nephews, and nieces, her mother, her husband, her in-laws. All gone. Even the remnants of the resistance, those few left after the uprising, have dispersed into the Polish countryside. She is more alone than she could have ever imagined. Only she knows her real name and she is perhaps dying. She is thirty years old.

I am over three years old. I have no consciousness of our danger, our separateness from the others. I have no awareness that we are playing a part. I only know that I have a special name, that I have been named for the Goddess of Peace. And each night, I sleep secure in that knowledge. And when I wet my bed, my mother places me on her belly and lies on the stain. She fears the old woman and hopes her body's warmth will dry the sheet before dawn.

My mother is walking down a road. Another woman joins her. My mother sees through the deception, but she has promised herself that never, under any circumstances, will she take that risk. So she swallows her hunger for contact and trust and instead talks about the sick child left behind and lies about the husband in the labor camp.

Someone is walking towards them. A large, strange woman with wild red hair. They try not to look at her too closely, to seem overly curious. But as they pass her, my mother feels something move inside her. The movement grows and grows till it is an explosion of yearning that she cannot contain. She stops, orders her companion to continue without her. And then she turns.

The woman with the red hair has also stopped and turned. She is grotesque, bloated with hunger, almost savage in her rags. She and my mother move towards each other. Cautiously, deliberately, they probe past the hunger, the swollen flesh, the infected skin, the rags. Slowly, they begin to pierce five years of encrusted history. And slowly, there is perception and recognition.

In this wilderness of occupied Poland, in this vast emptiness where no one can be trusted, my mother has suddenly, bizarrely, met one of my father's teachers. A family friend. Another Jew.

They do not cry, but weep as they chronicle the dead and count the living. Then they rush to me. To the woman I am a familiar sight. She calculates that I will not live out the week, but comments only on my striking resemblance to my father. She says she has contacts. She leaves. One night a package of food is delivered anonymously. We eat. We begin to bridge the gap towards life. We survive.

2. Chicago, 1964: I am walking home alone at midnight.

I am walking home alone at midnight. I am a student of literature, and each night I stay in the library until it closes. Yet each night, as I return I still feel unprepared for the next day. The nature of literary movements eludes me. I only understand individual writers. I have trouble remembering genre definitions, historical dates and names, cannot grasp their meaning, significance. A whole world of abstractions and theories remains beyond my reach, on the other side of a wall I cannot climb over.

So each night, I walk home clutching my books as if I were a small school child. The city is alien. Since coming to America, this is my first time away from a Jewish neighborhood, Jewish friends, and I feel isolated, baffled at how to make a place for myself in this larger, gentile world which I have entered.

I am walking home alone at midnight. The university seems an island ungrounded. Most of its surrounding streets have been emptied. On some, all evidence of previous life removed except for occasional fringes of rubble that reveal vague outlines that hint at things that were. On others, old buildings still stand, though these are hollow like caves, once of use and then abandoned. Everything is poised. Everything is waiting for the emptiness to close in on itself, for the emptiness to be filled up, for the emptiness to be swallowed and forgotten.

Walking home, I am only dimly aware of the meaning of this strange void through which I pass. I am even less aware of the dangers for someone like me, a woman walking home alone at midnight. I am totally preoccupied with another time, another place. Night after night, protected by the darkness, I think only of Elza who is dead. I am trying to place a fact about her, a fact which stubbornly resists classification: nothing that happened to her afterwards mattered. All the agonized effort. All that caring. *None of that mattered!*

At the end of the war, friends come to claim her. With the cold, calculated cunning of an adult, the eight year old vehemently denies who she is. No she is not who they think. Not a Jew. They have made a mistake. Mixed her up with another Elza. This one belongs here, with her mother.

She is simply being scrupulous in following her parents' instructions. "Do not ever admit to anyone who you are. It is our secret. Eventually we will come for you. Remember! *Never admit who you are!* Promise!"

Four years later, the war is over. Her parents are dead. She is still bound by her promise. This woman is her mother. Her parents' friends know better. The woman has been kind, has saved her. But she is a Pole and Elza is a Jew. Finally, the bribe is big enough and the child released. Elza becomes an orphan.

And afterwards? She is adopted and finally seems to have everything. Two parents. Two handsome brothers. A house. Her own room. She studies Latin and does translations. Is valedictorian of her class. Goes away to college. Has boyfriends, affairs. Comes to New York. Works. Begins graduate school. Explicates Dylan Thomas, T.S. Eliot. Marries.

But none of it matters. She cannot keep up. The signs are clear. She is a poor housekeeper. Insists they eat off paper plates. She buys enough clothes to fill all her closets. But nothing soothes her. Finally she signs her own papers. Is released within a few months. I finish college and leave for Europe. Three weeks later, she checks into a hotel and takes an overdose. She is twenty-five years old.

Fearing I too might be in danger, my mother instructs Polish Jews resettled in Paris and Tel Aviv: "Don't tell her!" And to me she writes: "Elza is in the hospital again. There is no hope." I am suspicious, refer to her whenever I can. I am alert. Sense a discomfort, an edge I cannot define. I think I know, but I never dare ask. I come home. Seven months after her death, I finally know.

A story she once told me remains alive. During the war, the Polish woman sends her to buy a notebook for school. She is given the wrong change and points it out. The shopkeeper eyes her sharply: "Very accurate. Just like a Jew. Perhaps you are a little Jewess?" And Elza feels afraid and wonders if this woman sees the truth in her blue eyes.

Another memory. Elza is reading accounts of the war. She cannot help herself she tells me. An anecdote explains something to her. A woman in a camp requests a bandage for a wound. And the guard, so startled by her simplicity and directness, makes sure she gets one. That woman, Elza tells me, refused to stop acting like a human being. Jews, she concludes, made a terrible mistake.

I am walking home alone at midnight. I am raw with the pain of her death. I wonder. Is it inevitable? Everything that happened to us afterwards, to all of us, does none of it matter? Does it not matter what we do and where we live? Are there moments in history which cannot be escaped or transcended, but which act like time warps permanently trapping all those who are touched by them? And that which should have happened in 1944 in Poland and didn't, must it happen now? In 1964? In Chicago? Or can history be tricked and cheated?

These questions haunt me. Yet I persist with a will I myself do not understand. I continue reading, studying, making friends. And as the rawness of Elza's death eases and becomes familiar, as time becomes distance, I find myself more and more grounded in my present life, in my passion for words and literature. I begin to perceive the world around me. I develop perspective.

I see the rubble of this unbombed landscape, see that the city, like the rest of this alien country, is not simply a geographic place, but a time zone, an era in which I, by my very presence in it, am rooted. No one simply passes through. History keeps unfolding and demanding a response. A life obliterated around me of those I barely noticed. A life unmarked, unrecorded. A silent mass migration. Relocation. Common rubble in the streets.

I see now the present dangers, the dangers of the void, of the American hollowness in which I walk calmly day and night as I continue my life. I begin to see the incessant grinding down of lines for stamps, for jobs, for a bed to sleep in, of a death stretched imperceptibly over a lifetime. I begin to understand the ingenuity of it. The invisibility. The Holocaust without smoke.

Everything is poised. Everything is waiting for the emptiness to be filled up, for the filling-up that can never replace, that can only take over. Like time itself. Or history.

3. Brooklyn, 1971: I am almost equidistant from two continents.

I am almost equidistant from two continents. I look back towards one, then forward towards the other. The moment is approaching when I will be equidistant from both and will have to choose. Maintaining equidistance is not a choice.

By one of those minor and peculiar coincidences that permanently shape and give texture to our lives, I am born on my father's twenty-eighth birthday. Two years later, exactly three days after his thirtieth and my second birthday, he is dead in the brush factory district of the Warsaw Ghetto. His corpse is buried in a courtyard and eventually the spot blends with the rest of the rubble. The Uprising, my birth, his death—all merge and become interchangeable. That is the heritage of one continent.

In one of the classes that I teach, all the students are Black and Puerto Rican. I am the only white. Initially, the students are nervous, wondering if I will be a hard taskmaster. I am nervous too, though I do not yet have a name for it. After a few months together, we grow accustomed to each other. I am trying to understand my role here. That is the heritage of the other continent.

And now, approaching my own thirtieth birthday, approaching the moment when I will be equidistant from the two land masses, I feel some kind of cellular breakdown in my body, a sudden surging inside me, as if flesh and muscle and bone were losing definition. Everything in me yearns to become transparent, to be everywhere, to become like the water between two vast land masses that will never touch. I desire to become salt water, to establish the connection.

I am almost equidistant from two continents.

April 17, 1955. I have been asked to light one of the six candles. I stand on the stage in the large, darkened auditorium, wait to be called, wait to accept the flame, to pass it on like a memory. I am numb with terror at the spectacle around me. I fear these people with blue numbers on their arms, people who are disfigured and scarred, who have missing limbs and uneasy walks, people whose histories repel me. Here in this auditorium, they abandon all inhibitions, they transform themselves into pure sound, the sound of irretrievable loss, of wild pain and sorrow. Then they become all flesh, wringing their hands and covering their swollen eyes and flushed faces. They call out to me and I feel myself dissolving.

When it is time for me to come forward, to light the candle for those children who were burned, who were shot, who were stomped to death, I move without feeling. And as I near the candelabra, I hear them call out the common Yiddish names: *Surele. Moyshele. Channele. Rivkele. Yankele. Shayndele. Rayzl. Benyo-min. Chavele. Miriam. Chaim.* The names brush against my face, invade my ears, my mouth. I breathe them into my lungs, into my bones. And as the list continues, guided by their sounds, I cross the stage and light the sixth and final candle. It is my fourteenth birthday.

I am almost equidistant from two continents.

March, 1971. There are twenty-eight people in the class. Eighteen women, ten men. Some married. Some single. Alone. With children. With parents and grandparents. Nieces. Nephews. They are here because they have not met the minimum standards of this college. This class is their special chance to catch up. Subject and verb agreement. Sentence fragments. Pronoun reference. Vocabulary building. Paragraph organization. Topic sentence. Reading comprehension. Study skills. Discipline. All this to catch up, or as one student said to me, his eyes earnest: "I want to write so that when I go for a job they won't think I'm lazy."

I am required to take attendance. I check through the names, call them out each morning: *James. Reggie. Marie. Simone. Joy. Christine.*

Alvarez. Ashcroft. Basile. Colon. Corbett. White. Raphael. Dennis. Juan. Carissa. Lamont. Andrea. Fragments of their lives fall before me. The chaos and disorganization. A mother needing help in filling out forms in English. A sick child. Hospital regulations. A brother looking for a job. Another brother in trouble. Welfare red tape. Unemployment payment restrictions. Waiting lists. Eviction. SRO. The daily grind interrupting their catching-up, and the increasing sense that with each day missed, they fall further behind.

I am almost equidistant from two continents. I look back towards one, then forward towards the other. There is a need in me to become transparent like water, to become the salt water which is their only connection.

March, 1971. Marie wants to study medicine. She concedes it's a long haul, but, as she says, "It's only time. What difference does it make?" Slightly older than the others, she lives alone with her daughter. To some of the women's horror, she refuses to have a telephone, does not like to be intruded upon. When necessary, she can always be reached through a neighbor. She rarely misses class, on a few occasions brings her daughter with her who sits serenely drawing pictures. Facing Marie, I sometimes do not know who I am and wonder how she perceives me. She seems oblivious to my discomfort. She is only focused on the class, always reworking her assignments, reading everything twice, asking endless questions to make sure she really understands. One day, at the end of the hour, when we are alone, she asks: "What are you?" I am caught off guard, know the meaning of the question, but feel the resistance in me. I break it down and answer quietly: "A Jew." She nods and in that moment two vast land masses touch.

Each continent has its legacy. The day I reach my thirtieth birthday, the age of my father's death, I am equidistant from both. And as the moment passes, everything in me becomes defined again. I am once again muscle, flesh, bone. America is not my chosen home, not even the place of my birth. Just a spot where it seemed safe to go to escape certain dangers. But safety, I discover, is only temporary. No place guarantees it to anyone forever. I have stayed because there is no other place to go. In my muscles, my flesh, my bone, I balance the heritages, the histories of two continents.

4. Cherry Plain: I have become a keeper of accounts.

There are moments when I suddenly become breathless, as if I had just tricked someone, but was afraid the ruse would be exposed and I'd be hunted again. At those moments, the myths that propel our history, that turn fiction into fact, emerge in full force in me, as I stare into the eyes of strangers or someone suddenly grown alien. And when I see their eyes become pinpoints of judgments, become cold and indifferent, or simply distanced with curiosity, at those moments I hear again the words of the Polish woman:

Very accurate. Just like a Jew. You are perhaps a little Jewess?

At moments such as these I teeter, shed the present, and like rage, like pride, like acceptance, like the refusal to deny, I call upon the ancient myths again and say:

Yes. It's true. All true. I am scrupulously accurate. I keep track of all distinctions. Between past and present. Pain and pleasure. Living and surviving. Resistance and capitulation. Will and circumstances. Between life and death. Yes. I am scrupulously accurate. I have become a keeper of accounts.

Like the patriarchs, the shabby scholars who only lived for what was written and studied it all their lives

Like the inhuman usurers and dusty pawnbrokers who were quarantined within precisely prescribed limits of every European town and who were as accurate as the magistrates that drew the boundaries of their lives and declared them diseased

Like those men of stone who insisted that the *goyim* fulfill the contracts they had signed and who responded to the tearful pleas of illness, weakness, sudden calamity and poverty, with the words: "What are these to me? You have made me a keeper of accounts.

Give me my pound of flesh. It says on this piece of paper, you owe me a pound of flesh!"

Like those old, heartless, dried up merchants whose entire lives were spent in the grubby *shtetl* streets that are now but memory, whose only body softness was in their fingertips worn smooth by silver coins, whose vision that all that mattered was on pieces of paper was proven absolutely accurate, when their zloty, francs, and marks could not buy off the written words *Żyd, Juif, Jüde*

Like these, my despised ancestors
I have become a keeper of accounts.

And like all the matriarchs, the wives and daughters, the sisters and aunts, the nieces, the keepers of button shops, milliners, seam-stresses, peddlers of foul fish, of matches, of rotten apples, laun-dresses, midwives, floor washers and street cleaners, who rushed exhausted all week so that *shabes* could be observed with fresh *khalah* on the table, who argued in the common tongue

and begged for the daughter run off to the revolution
and the daughter run off with a *sheygets*
who refused to sit *shiva* and say *kadish* for a living child
who always begged for life
who understood the accounts but saw them differently
who knew the power of human laws, knew they always counted
no matter what the revolution or the party or the state
who knew the power of the words *Żyd, Juif, Jüde*

who cried whole lifetimes for their runaway children
for the husbands immobilized by the written word
for the brother grown callous from usury
for the uncle grown indifferent from crime, from bargaining,
from chiseling, from jewing them down

Like these, my despised ancestors
I have become a keeper of accounts.

I do not shun this legacy. I claim it as mine   whenever I see the
photographs of nameless people. Standing staring off the edge of
the picture. People dressed in coats lined with fur. Or ragged at
elbows and collar. Hats cocked on one side glancing anxiously
toward the lens. A peasant cap centered and ordinary. Hair styled
in the latest fashion. Or standing ashamed a coarse wig awk-
wardly fitted. The shabby clothes. Buttons missing. The elegant
stance. Diamond rings. Gold teeth. The hair being shaved. The
face of humiliation. The hand holding the child's hand. A tree. A
track. A vague building in a photograph. A facility. And then the
fields of hair   the endless fields of hair   the earth growing fertile
with their bodies   with their souls.

Old   rarely seen types. Gone   they say   forever. And yet I
know they can be revived again   that I can trigger them again.
That they awaken in me   for I have felt it happen   in the sight
of strangers   or someone suddenly grown alien. Whenever I have
seen the judgment   the coldness   and indifference   the
distanced curiosity.   At those moments   I teeter   shed my
present self   and all time merges   and like rage   like pride
like acceptance   like the refusal to deny   I answer

Yes. It is true.   I am a keeper of accounts.

Bashert

200

Solitary Acts

for my aunt Gina Klepfisz (1908?-1942)

To garden is a solitary act.
         —Michelle Cliff

1.

And to die
as you did   with the father
confessor   standing   waiting
patiently   for your death
for your final words
and you   watching the dissolution
around you   watching his eyes
his face   listening to his Latin words
said: "What have I to confess?
I am a Jew."

It was 1942   and you wanted someone
to know   though you'd be buried
in a Christian grave   with an Aryan name.

Such will to be known   can alter history.

2.

Today   I stand alone   planning my first garden
and think of you   buried on that other continent
rescued from the Christian plot
the only flesh of your family   to lie
in a marked grave   in the Jewish cemetery
in a Warsaw   almost empty of any Jews.
That ground   I know   is but a fragment
of the past   a place apart   the surroundings
long rebuilt   into a modern city
and I know   that even now
while I stand   and try to map this season's growth
that country   cleansed of our people's blood
intones the litany of old complaints.

Gina   they hate us still.

3.

You are to me   everything
that remains   outside my grasp
everything   in this world
that is destroyed   with no one
there to rescue the fragments
to hear the words.
So much of history   seems
a gaping absence   at best a shadow
longing   for some greater
definition   which will never come
for what is burned   becomes air
and ashes   nothing more.

So I cling   to the knowledge of your
distant grave   for it alone
reminds me   prods me   to shape that shadow.

4.

I have spent a life   disentangling from influences
trying to claim   what was original   mine:
from my mother's mastery   of daily survival
so subtly interwoven   with common gestures
few recognize it   for what it is
from my father's more visibly   heroic deed
of dying   recorded in memoirs   tributes
from the deaths of grandparents   aunts   uncles
anonymous   in a heap   indistinguishable
from all the others   who died unmourned.

And now I remember you   and face another:
Gina   in those few months   when you watched
over me   before my consciousness learned
the danger   into which I had just been born
and the label   of who I was   and while my mother
sick and weak   teetered on the edge of life
in those few months   as the meaning of the ghetto
walls   grew more defined   as you inched people
out of the *umschlagplatz*   your chest contracting
gasping   with fear   yet certain that this needed to be done
I believe   that in that short time   something
passed between us   Gina   and you imparted to me
the vision   the firm sense of self   that gave
you strength   to state your name.

5.

And who would say   that I have mourned
enough   that I have looked at the old
photographs enough   yellowed and faded
and the green ink   now a grey dullness
where Marek   placed the flowers
on the rubble   where my father's body
was buried and disappeared   and Marek's head
looking down   his profile   etched against
an empty horizon   for there was nothing left

who would say   that I have mourned
enough?

And when I asked my mother if I
could have this album   that holds it all
holds more than most have   who are
without a witness   to mark their spot in green
or whose graves have been overgrown by weeds
or forests   or bulldozed for the sake
of modern cities   or whose bodies were never
buried   but were left for speechless animals
to devour   there is no piece of earth
that does not have its nameless   who lived
and died   unnoticed   beyond the grasp of history
who die today

And when I asked my mother   if I
could have this album   and she replied
this stays here   in this apartment
until I die   I glimpsed again the urgency
to be known.

6.

There have been many plots of ground
that formed me. This town's church
its cemetery   the bare   expectant earth
of my garden   all remind me   of that
other soil   on which I grew.

The first   was the green bush and grass
behind Marek's house in Lodz. It was
after the war   and Elza   orphaned   and just recently
claimed   from the Polish stranger   stood proud
before me   and brushed her long blond hair
her haughtiness   her only power. I watched
ashamed   and awkward   my small hand trying
to hide   my bald head   shaved for reasons
I was never told. It was our first meeting.

More than two years later   in the neutral
countryside that never saw the war   in Neglinge
Gaby and I   crawled flat on our stomachs
to see the miniature wild flowers   hidden
beneath the blooming lilac bush. They grew
for elves   I said   and bound him to me
with the secret   not wanting anyone else
to know. He was alert then   but only months
before   had refused to eat   was force fed
in a Stockholm hospital. When his appetite
returned   he clung to me   four years older
in a way   no one could ever understand
and I responded   as I never would again
unconsciously   selflessly   with complete
certainty.   I knew that he must live
and inched him along.

And again   a few years later   in a park   the Bronx
there was an unmowed field   near a metal fence.
My mother would bring me here   on warm summer Sundays
and spread a blanket   that would billow
over the high   resistant grass   then finally settle
and flatten with the weight of our bodies.
We brought things to read   books that warmed
with the sun   newspapers   that yellowed
as the day wore on.

These were the gardens of my childhood.

7.

Gina   I must tell you: today I
felt hopeful   as I knelt close
to the earth   and turned it
inch by inch   sifting the soil
clearing the way   for roots
of vegetables. I felt so hopeful
Gina   that with repeated years
and efforts   the monotony of daily
motion   of bending   and someday
the earth   would be uncluttered
the debris cleared.

There is   I know   no reason
for such hope   for nothing destroyed
is ever made up   or restored to us.
In the earth   are buried histories
irretrievable.   Yet what philosophy
can justify   any of our emotions?
Like the watercolors from Buchenwald—
if you can imagine! The stench
from the chimneys   just the sounds
of the place. And yet someone felt
a need to paint. And did.

So do not ask me to explain
why I draw meaning and strength
from these common gestures   why today
my hope is unwavering   solid   as if
I'd never lost it   or never would again
as if those dying   angry or stunned
at the stupidity of it   could be revived
as if their mortal wounds   could heal

as if their hunger   could be outlived
as if they were not dying   strangers
to others   strangers to themselves.

I need to hope. And do.

8.

I have been a dreamer   dreaming
of a perfect garden   of a family tree
whose branches   spread   through centuries
of an orderly cemetery   with no gravestones
missing.   Tonight   as the sun sets   and I
turn towards evening   I have no such dreams.
Like the woman   who refused to trace
the ancient constellations   upon a clear
and crowded sky   because finding the stars
recording each in its place   the faint
and the brilliant   was enough
I too   Gina   have discarded all patterns
and blueprints. This night   I want only
to sleep   a dark   rich   dreamless sleep
to shelter   in me   what is left
to strengthen myself   for what is needed.

Cherry Plain, New York
August 1982

A Few Words
in the Mother Tongue

New Poems (1983 - 1990)

I cannot swim

I cannot swim   but my parents
say the land is less safe.   And
the first day   the water was smooth
like slate I could walk on.
It was a deception.

The sky greyed   darkened
then grew bright as if it understood
our mood.   I watched the land sink
and disappear. The boat was firm.
I sat holding onto my father's leg.
I was not sick like the others.

The sky was bright   then grew
grey and dark. The days were
the same   the water the same
and everyone's eyes the same.
We looked like a family but
we were all strangers.   Nothing
but water and sky and the boat.
The world never existed I said.
I could not remember land   nor
houses nor trees and I knew
I had not been born here
that once there had been another place.
And I said to my parents:
there are no more lands
and no more peoples.   We are strange
creatures and must grow gills.
And my parents laughed as I cupped
my hands around my ears and the
children laughed and did the same
their bony fingers flapping.

And the water looked gentle
ready to receive us.

And one day   we saw them   and I
saw we were not alone   and there
were others. Not sea creatures
but like us. I remembered.
And they boarded us   and seized
the young girls like me   and formed
a circle.   And they were on us
when the leader shouted: Make
sounds of joy!   And my parents' eyes
sealed like wrinkled walnuts.
And they changed places   and new ones
were on us.   And someone ordered:
Make sounds of joy!   My parents moved
their lips like fishes   their mouths
filled with silence.   And it happened
again and again   to me   till I stopped
remembering it.

The blood clotted between the boards
and darkened   though the women splashed
the sea on it.   The smell stayed.
I said to my parents: I will grow gills
and tried to leap out   into the water.
But my father held my wrists   his fingers
iron nails piercing my bones.   And he said:
you cannot swim.

The ocean was bleak and jagged
like an unscaled mountain   daring
to be conquered.   At dusk someone
spotted the land   but I did not look
at it   and watched my shadow below
on the rippled darkening bottom.

I thought about those who waited
on the shore. They were shouting
sharp   not kind   pointing at an empty
horizon.   Wood splintered wood   just
for one moment   and then they pushed
us back. My mother pressed my head
against her breast. The day was ending.
It was almost dark.

Di rayze aheym / The journey home

1. *Der fentster* / The window

She looks out the window.
All is present.
The shadows of the past
fall elsewhere.

This is the wilderness
she thinks.

And our tongues have become
dry   the wilderness has
dried out our tongues   and
we have forgotten speech.

She looks out the window.
All is present.

2. *Vider a mol* / Once again

Vider a mol
she tries to rise above circumstances.

Too much is at stake
this morning
yedn frimorgn
          every morning
to see what can be wrenched
from the unconscious
crowded darkness
fun ir zikorn
          of her memory.

It is there
di gantse geshikhte
fun folk
          the entire history
of the people.

Vider a mol
          she reaches out
and tries to hold on
clinging
          like a drowning
person
     to a flimsy plank.

Ober der yam iz groys
but the sea is vast
un di velt
       and the world
afile greser
         even larger
            afile greser.

3. *Zi flit* / She flies

Zi flit
vi a foygl
>> like a bird
zi flit
ibern yam
>> over the sea
iber di berg
>> over the mountains.

Tsurik
> *tsurik* back
>> back

zi flit
> and settles
oyf a boym
>> on a tree
lebn a moyer
>> near a wall

a moyer
fun a beys-oylem
>> a wall
>> of a cemetery.

4. *A beys-oylem* / A cemetery

Der moyer   the wall

oyf der zayt

           on this side

un oyf der zayt

           and on this side

Oyf beyde zaytn   on both sides.

Oyf der zayt
a keyver

           on this side

a grave

           oyf der zayt
           a vistenish

on this side

           a wasteland.

Der moyer
a beys-oylem
oyf der zayt

           un oyf der zayt.

5. *Kashes* / Questions

In velkhn yor?

        in what year

Mit vemen?

        with whom?

Di sibes?

        the causes?

Der rezultat?

        the outcome?

di geshikhte

        the history

fun der milkhome

        of the war

fun dem sholem

        of the peace

fun di lebn geblibene

        of the survivors

tsvishn fremde

        among strangers

oyf der zayt

        on this side

        tsvishn meysim

among ghosts

        oyf der zayt

on this side.

6. *Zi shemt zihk*/She is ashamed

Zi shemt zikh.

> She has forgotten
> *alts fargesn*

forgotten it all.

> Whom can I speak to?
> she wonders.

di mame	the mother
der tate	the father
di bobe	the grandmother
der zeyde	the grandfather
di oves	the ancestors

alts
alts fargesn
forgotten it all

> *di gantse mishpokhe*
> the entire family

dos folk
the people

> *Mit vemen*
> *ken ikh redn?*
> Whom can I speak to?

di meysim farshteyen
mir afile nit
> even the ghosts
> do not understand me.

7. *In der fremd* / Among strangers

Vi azoy?   how
                  she wonders
                  should I speak?

                  Velkhe verter
which words
should I use
in der fremd
                  among strangers?

Zog
bloyz dem emes
                  speak
                  only the truth
kayn lign nit
                  no lies.

Zi gedenkt
She remembers
di lektsyes
                  the lessons
di printsipn
                  the principles

                  un zi shvaygt
and she remains

                  silent.

8. *Di tsung* / The tongue

Zi shvaygt.

Di verter feln ir
she lacks the words
and all that she can force

is sound
unformed sound:

a
der klang

        the sound

o
dos vort

        the word

u
di tsung

        the tongue

o
dos loshn

        the language

e
di trern

        the tears.

9. *Di rayze aheym* / The journey home

Zi flit

> she flies

vi a foygl

> like a bird

vi a mes

> like a ghost

Zi flit
iber di berg

> over the mountains

ibern yam

> over the sea.

Tsurik

> *tsurik* back
>
>> back

In der fremd

> among strangers

iz ir heym

> is her home.

> *Do*

here
ot do

> right here

muz zi lebn

> she must live.

Ire zikhroynes

> her memories
> will become monuments

ire zikhroynes
will cast shadows.

Etlekhe verter oyf mame-loshn/
A few words in the mother tongue

lemoshl: for example

di kurve   the whore
a woman who acknowledges her passions

di yidene   the Jewess   the Jewish woman
ignorant   overbearing
let's face it: every woman is one

di yente   the gossip   the busybody
who knows what's what
and is never caught off guard

di lezbianke   the one with
a roommate   though we never used
the word

dos vaybl   the wife
or the little woman

* * *

in der heym   at home
where she does everything to keep
yidishkayt alive

yidishkayt   a way of being
Jewish   always arguable

in mark   where she buys
di kartofl un khalah
(yes, potatoes and challah)

di kartofl   the material counter-
part of *yidishkayt*

mit tsibeles   with onions
that bring *trern tsu di oygn*
tears to her eyes   when she sees
how little it all is
veyniker un veyniker
less and less

di khalah   braided
vi ir hor far der khasene
like her hair before the wedding
when she was *aza sheyn meydl*
such a pretty girl

di lange shvartse hor
the long black hair
di lange shvartse hor

* * *

a froy kholmt   a woman
dreams *ir ort oyf der velt*
her place in this world
un zi hot moyre   and she is afraid
so afraid of the words

kurve
yidene
yente
lezbianke
vaybl

zi kholmt   she dreams
un zi hot moyre   and she is afraid
ir ort
di velt
di heym
der mark

a meydl kholmt
a kurve kholmt
a yidene kholmt
a yente kholmt
a lezbianke kholmt

a vaybl kholmt
di kartofl
di khalah

yidishkayt

zi kholmt
di hor
di lange shvartse hor

zi kholmt
zi kholmt
zi kholmt

Fradel Schtok

Yiddish writer. B. 1890 in Skale, Galicia. Emigrated to New York in 1907. Became known when she introduced the sonnet form into Yiddish poetry. Author of *Erzeylungen* (Stories) in 1919, a collection in Yiddish. Switched to English and published *For Musicians Only* in 1927. Institutionalized and died in a sanitarium around 1930.

Language is the only homeland.
      —Czeslow Milosz

They make it sound easy: some disjointed
sentences   a few allusions   to
mankind.   But for me   it was not
so simple   more like   trying
to cover the distance   from here
to the corner   or between two sounds.

Think of it: *heym*   and   *home*   the meaning
the same   of course   exactly
but the shift   in vowel   was the ocean
in which I drowned.

I tried.   I did   try.
First held with Yiddish   but you
know   it's hard.   You write   *gas*
and   *street*   echoes back
No resonance.   And—let's face it—
memory falters.
You try to keep track of the difference
like *got* and *god*   or *hoyz* and *house*
but they blur   and you start using
alley   when you mean *gesele*   or *avenue*
when it's a *bulevar*.

And before you know it
you're on   some alien path
standing   before a brick house
the doorframe   slightly familiar.
Still   you can't place it
exactly.   Passers-by stop.
Concerned   they speak   but you've
heard   all this   before the vowels
shifting   up and down   the subtle
change   in the guttural sounds
and now   it's nothing more
nothing   more   than   babble.
And so   you accept it.
You're lost.   This time   you really
don't know   where you are.

Land or sea   the house floats before you.
Perhaps you once sat   at that window
and it was home   and looked out
on that *street* or *gesele*.   Perhaps
it was a dead end   perhaps a short cut.
Perhaps not.
A movement by the door.   They stand there
beckoning   mouths open and close:
Come in! Come in!   I understood   it was
a welcome.   *A dank! A dank!*
I said   till I heard the lock
snap   behind me.

Der mames shabosim /
My Mother's Sabbath Days

Inspired by Vella Grade in Chaim Grade's memoir

Bay undz is es geven andersh.   I knew nothing
of the 613 *mitsves*   which did not bind me   nor
of the 3 which did   though I am sure my grandmother
Rikla Perczykow   knew them all   and I have a vague
image   of her covering her eyes   and swaying.

Shoshana   Różka   Lodzia   Mamma Lo   and more recently
Rose   in short: my mother   in all her reincarnations
did not pass on   such things.
She'd given them up   even before she'd ever claimed them.
She was more modern   and besides   there were other matters
to teach   so by age 11   *kh'bin shoyn geven a brenendike sotsyalistke*
I was a passionate socialist   impatient   so impatient
to grow   into my knowledge   never guessing
there was no choice   for work   and rest   wrestled
in every human life   with work   inevitably
the unbeatable winner.

So for us it was different.   *Erev shabes*   was plain   *fraytik*
or more precisely: *piontek.*   I remember   summer evenings
I'd wait for her   at the Mosholu stop of the Lexington line.
Bright heat and light   at 6 o'clock.   She was full
of tales   of Miss Kant   the designer   a career woman
longing for home and family   in love with a handsome pilot
of Scottie   the model   who married smart   a wealthy buyer
and now sat brazenly chic   in a reform synagogue.
I listened   eager   to understand these   widow tales   of romance
amid the rush   of each season's showing   and once   even
saw   on a page of the *Times*   a mannequin   dressed in
the very gown   Mamma Lo had made.

All the way up Jerome Avenue   we'd walk   past the Jewish deli
where we never ate   (what was the point if you could make it at home?)
past the pizza place   where occasionally   while shopping   she'd buy me
a slice   past the outdoor groceries   fruit stands   fabric   shoes
lingerie   and stationery stores—till Gun Hill Road   and Jade Gardens.
Perhaps I knew it was *treyf*.   She certainly did
but was not concerned.   We'd order   the salty wonton soup
chow mein   or pepper steak   and though she mocked the food
she never resisted.
It was Friday.   The shop was closed.   We'd eat dinner and like the rich
lean leisurely back in our booth.   I didn't know it was *erev shabes*.
Still—she rested.

'67 Remembered

for Khane

In '67 you visited with your sister.
I was in Chicago.   Richard Speck had just murdered
seven nurses.   We were scared.   The war was only
a few days over   and everyone said
how well you and Gitl looked.   Who would
have thought   you'd just come
from a war-torn country
dressed chic   in late '60s fashion
smiling   easy   relaxed
confident   the worst was over?
I still have the photographs.

How different   that war
from that other   in your life:
Siberia   the Germans at your heels
your father chopping trees in the forest.
You learned Russian in the street
spoke Yiddish at home   wrote Polish
in the segregated schools.   You were
a linguist at eight   ready to master
even more tongues   for the sake of survival.

But in '67   you'd already mastered
it all.   You were so relaxed   so easy.
It was a joke   this war   despite
the casualties.   It was a joke
how relaxed   you were.

And wasn't I too?   Weren't we all?
Didn't we all glow from it

our sense of power finally achieved?
The quickness of the action
the Biblical routes
and how we laughed over
Egyptian shoes in the sand
how we laughed at another people's fear
as if fear was alien
as if we had known safety   all our lives.

And the Bank?
I don't remember   it mentioned
by any of us.
We were in Chicago—it was hard to imagine.
But twenty years later
I hear how they picked up what they could
placed it on their backs
how they marched through the hills
sparse   coarse grass   pink and yellow flowers
rough rocks   defying cultivation
how they carried   clumsy packs
clothing   utensils   images of a home
they might   never see again.
A sabra told me   who watched
their leaving as she sat safe
in an army jeep: it looked no different
than the newsreels at school
of French   Belgian roads. It was simple
she said: people were fleeing   and
we egged them on.

Time passes.   Everything changes.
We see things differently.
In '67 you had not married yet   and we all
wondered why   never worrying about
marriage laws   or rabbinic power.

And now more than 20 years later
you live in Jerusalem   ruling
from your lacquered kitchen   and sit
in that dream house   trapped:
enough food   in your mouth
in your children's   and enough warm things
for winter   (coats   shoes   woolen stockings
good for Siberia)
and there's no way out   no one to call
about a bad marriage.   It's simple:
a woman   without bruises
your lawyer says   there's not much hope
and you accept it:
I can't say I'm happy   but
I've got a truce.

Things fester.   We compromise.
We wake up   take new positions
to suit new visions   failed dreams.
We change.   Power does not so much corrupt
as blur the edges
so we no longer feel   the raw fear
that pounds in the hearts
of those trapped   and helpless.
In '67 in Chicago   we thought we'd be safe
locking the windows   till Speck was caught.
We did not know   there was a danger
in us as well   that we must remain vigilant
and open   not to power
but to peace.

Warsaw, 1983: *Umschlagplatz*

In Treblinke bin ikh nit geven.
I was never in Treblinka.
                    —H. Leivik

No horrors this time.
It's 1983.   June.   Summer.
Warsaw is tense   but over *Solidarność*
over amnesty.

A small white brick wall.
Two plaques in Polish   and Yiddish
to the effect   that from here
zaynen zey geforn kayn Treblinke.
Two stubby candles on either side
neither burning.   The guide
lights one with a lighter.
The wind blows it out.

A gas station pumping gas
right behind.   A building on
one side.   Perhaps   from that time
efsher an eydes.   Maybe it saw.
And there are tracks
I think.

Umschlagplatz (German)—Place of deportation for concentration
camps, in this case, Treblinka.

I do not cry.   What's to cry
about?   An ordinary street.
People   going about
their business forty years later
tense about amnesty.

This street might have been my home.
This street might have been the beginning
of my journey to death.
I must remember:
it was neither.

I live on another continent.
It is 1983.   I am now a visitor.
History stops for no one.

East Jerusalem, 1987:
Bet Shalom (House of Peace)

In 1987 in East Jerusalem a group of Jewish women writers (American and Israeli) met with Palestinian women to express feelings and responses to the Israeli occupation of the West Bank and Gaza. I was very moved by this meeting, but could not write about it until after the *intifada* had begun. I was particularly affected by one of the Palestinian women, to whom this poem is dedicated.

To a Palestinian woman who I am afraid to name

Whether we like it or not
we must sit here.   What we feel
does not matter.   We are the heirs:
our legacy is in the air we breathe
the ground we stand on.

One of us lives   in the neighborhood
you were raised in
where you took   your first steps
and met the world.
Then everyone left.
Your uncles and aunts
carried their belongings
and left.   It was '48.

You ask us:

> *Do you understand   can you imagine*
> *what it must feel like to me?*
> *To all of us?*
> *I do not go back to those neighborhoods.*

I just don't feel right.
Do you understand
what it means to all of us?

We understand   we remember history
and understand it all:
the need for safety   a safety
no one else can take away.
The need for control
not waiting on line   to get attention
or for the consciences of others   to awaken.
We understand what it means to have children
who die   children who live and learn to be proud
of who they are.

Doubts   break through.
This is in the air   the reluctance
to have understanding be enough.
We ask: didn't you omit
part of the picture
didn't you leave out a piece   along the border
a piece of the sky   the very peak of a mountain
the bus bombed   the children in the schoolhouse
peaceful farmers   ploughing fields—
you left out part of the picture.

Understanding wraps us again   tightly
towards each other.
We remember the camps: during   and after.
During: there was murder   and resistance
more murder   *and after:*   there was determination
sneaking in at night   no lights burning
the small boats   the landings on the beach
when everyone else had said: don't go there

or there   or there   or who wants them anyway
they've always been trouble   *and again after:*
bombings   massacres
we understand   the actions of a desperate people.

Doubts break us apart
we can barely breathe. We ask:
why are you our problem too?   We can hardly hold
our own. Why can't you just blend in
with your own kind?

Whether we like it   or not
we must sit here   and this is in the air.
You say to us:
     You must understand
     how it is for me.
     You are writers.
     Write about it.
You mean: Our voices carry.
Yours alone does not.

All of us part. You move off in a separate
direction. The rest of us return
to the other Jerusalem. It is night.
I still hear your voice. It is in the air
now   with everything else   except sharper
clearer.   I think of your relatives
your uncles and aunts   I see the familiar
battered suitcases   cartons with strings
stuffed pillowcases
children sitting on people's shoulders
children running to keep up

Always   there is migration
on this restless planet   everywhere
there is displacement   somewhere
someone is always telling   someone else
to move on   to go elsewhere.

Night.   Jerusalem.   *Yerushalayim.*
Jerusalem.   If I forget thee
Oh Jerusalem   Jerusalem   Hebron
Ramallah   Nablus   Qattana   if I
forget thee oh Jerusalem
Oh Hebron   may I forget
my own past   my pain
the depth of my sorrows.

GLOSSARY AND REFERENCES

bay undz iz es geven andersh (Yiddish)—at our house it was different

bobe (Yiddish)—grandmother

khalah (Yiddish)—a braided egg bread eaten on the Sabbath

efsher an eydes (Yiddish)—perhaps a witness

erev shabes (Yiddish)—Friday night, Sabbath eve

fraytik (Yiddish)—Friday

goyim (Yiddish)—non-Jews, usually pejorative

Ich habe ein kleines kind. (German)—I have a small child.

intifada (Arabic)—Palestinian uprising in the West Bank and Gaza Strip which began December 9, 1987.

kadish (Yiddish)—a prayer for the dead

mame-loshn (Yiddish)—mother tongue; used synonymously to mean the Yiddish language

mitsves (Yiddish)—obligatory good deeds required of Jewish men (613) and women (3)

Neglinge—village outside of Stockholm, Sweden

Pan Tadeusz—Nineteenth-century national Polish epic by Adam Mickiewicz

piontek (Polish)—Friday

rebe (Yiddish)—rabbi

rebitsin (Yiddish)—rabbi's wife

Sabra (Hebrew)—a native-born Israeli

Solidarność (Polish)—Solidarity movement in Poland; illegal in 1983

shabes (Yiddish)—Sabbath

sheygets (Yiddish)—non-Jewish man, pejorative

shiva (Yiddish)—a seven-day mourning period for the dead

shtetl (Yiddish)—small Jewish towns and communities in Eastern Europe virtually destroyed by the end of World War II

treyf (Yiddish)—non-kosher

umschlagplatz (German)—place of deportation for concentration camps

zaynen zey geforn kayn Treblinke (Yiddish)—they went to Treblinka

zloty, francs, marks (Polish, French, German)—monetary units

Żyd, Juif, Jüde (Polish, French, German)—Jew

NOTES

In the transliteration of Yiddish words, I have followed the rules established by YIVO Institute for Jewish Research and generally accepted by international linguistic organizations. The YIVO guidelines have also been followed for the transliteration of Hebrew words used in Yiddish.

they're always curious

Although this poem did not appear in *periods of stress*, it is included here because it was written during the same time as many of the other poems in that collection. *periods of stress* was self-published, so the omission was due solely to my own "forgetfulness."

Contexts

I worked on "Contexts" over a six-month period and experienced great difficulty in pulling the sections together. Only after I had read Tillie Olsen's *Silences* was I able to see the relationship between the parts and complete the poem. Both epigraphs are taken from *Silences*.

Solitary Acts

"Like the watercolors from Buchenwald"—For the extraordinary artwork produced in ghettos, concentration camps and in hiding, see the reproductions in *The Art of the Holocaust*, Janet Blatter and Sybil Milton, eds. (New York: Rutledge Press, 1981).

Warsaw, 1983: *Umschlagplatz*

In Treblinke bin ikh nit geven is taken from the title poem of a collection by the Yiddish poet H. Leivik.

ABOUT THE AUTHOR

IRENA KLEPFISZ WAS BORN IN WARSAW, POLAND IN 1941 AND EMIGRATED to the United States in 1949. Educated in New York City public schools and Workmen's Circle Yiddish schools, she attended City College of New York and received her Ph.D. in English Literature from the University of Chicago. Over the past twenty years she has taught English, creative writing, Women's Studies, and Yiddish. An activist in the lesbian/feminist and Jewish communities, she was a founder of *Conditions*, a feminist magazine emphasizing the writing of lesbians, the co-editor of *A Tribe of Dina: A Jewish Woman's Anthology* and co-editor of *A Jewish Women's Call for Peace: A Handbook for Jewish Women on the Israeli/Palestinian Conflict*. She is the author of *Dreams of an Insomniac: Jewish Feminist Essays, Speeches and Diatribes*, which was published in 1990 by The Eighth Mountain Press as a companion volume to this one.

About the Cover Artist

Marcia Barrentine did the artwork and designed the cover for *A Few Words in the Mother Tongue*. She is a graphic designer and artist who lives in Portland, Oregon. The cover art is loosely based on designs found on Eastern European Jewish documents and artifacts.

About the Book

THE TEXT TYPOGRAPHY WAS COMPOSED IN PALATINO. THE COVER TYPOGRAPHY was composed in Seagull. The book was printed and bound by Baker Johnson on acid-free paper. *A Few Words in the Mother Tongue, Poems Selected and New (1971-1990)* has been issued in a first edition of five thousand of which five hundred are cloth-bound.